22nd SIGMORPHON Workshop on Computational Morphology, Phonology, and Phonetics

Albuquerque, New Mexico, USA
3 May 2025

ISBN: 979-8-3313-1929-8

Printed from e-media with permission by:

Curran Associates, Inc.
57 Morehouse Lane
Red Hook, NY 12571

CURRAN ASSOCIATES INC.
proceedings
.com

Some format issues inherent in the e-media version may also appear in this print version.

Printed with permission by Curran Associates, Inc. (2026)

Association for Computational Linguistics
209 N. Eighth Street
Stroudsburg, Pennsylvania 18360

Phone: 1-570-476-8006
Fax: 1-570-476-0860

acl@aclweb.org

Additional copies of this publication are available from:

Curran Associates, Inc.
57 Morehouse Lane
Red Hook, NY 12571 USA
Phone: 845-758-0400
Fax: 845-758-2633
Email: curran@proceedings.com
Web: www.proceedings.com

NAACL 2025

The 22nd SIGMORPHON workshop on Computational Morphology, Phonology, and Phonetics

Proceedings of the Workshop

May 3, 2025

Order copies of this and other ACL proceedings from:

Association for Computational Linguistics (ACL)
317 Sidney Baker St. S
Suite 400 - 134
Kerrville, TX 78028
USA
Tel: +1-855-225-1962
acl@aclweb.org

Organizing Committee

Co-Chair

Garrett Nicolai, University of British Columbia
Eleanor Chodroff, University of Zürich
Çagri Çöltekin, University of Tübingen
Fred Mailhot, Dialpad, Inc.

SIGMORPHON Officers

President: Garrett Nicolai, University of British Columbia
At Large: Eleanor Chodroff, University of Zürich
At Large: Çağrı Çöltekin, University of Tübingen
At Large: Fred Mailhot, Dialpad, Inc.

Program Committee

Michael Ginn, University of Colorado
Kenneth Steimel, Cisco Systems Incorporated
Sandra Kübler, Indiana University
Changbing Yang, University of British Columbia
Sarah Moeller, University of Florida
Rob Malouf, San Diego State University
Gregory Kobele, Leipzig University

Keynote Talk
Invited Talk

Kyle Gorman
City University of New York
2025-05-03 09:30:00 –

Abstract: The past and future of grapheme-to-phoneme conversion
I will describe three strands of recent work on grapheme-to-phoneme conversion (G2P). After introducing this task, I will briefly review some lessons learned from the SIGMORPHON 2020 and 2021 shared tasks on G2P. Then, I will focus on low-resource scenarios, describing in-progress work on unsupervised G2P using a decipherment framework and novel algorithms. Finally, I will turn to high-resource scenarios, describing in-progress work on what I am calling "grapheme-and-phoneme-to-phoneme conversion", in which "side pronunciations" from other dialects and/or transcription systems are provided as additional inputs to the G2P system to improve robustness and generalization.
Bio: Kyle Gorman is an associate professor at the Graduate Center, City University of New York, where he directs the master's program in computational linguistics. He is also a software engineer at Google Research. He is president and cofounder of the ACL Special Interest Group on Writing Systems and Written Language (SIGWrit). He is the coauthor of Finite-State Text Processing (Morgan & Claypool, 2021) and papers in computational linguistics and phonological theory.

Keynote Talk
Panel Discussion

Gasper Begus, Kyle Gorman, Connor Mayer, Kristine Yu
University of California Berkeley, City University of New York, University of Massachusetts Amherst, University of California Irvine
2025-05-03 13:30:00 –

Bio: Gašper Begus is an Associate Professor at the University of California, Berkeley, where he bridges the fields of linguistics, artificial intelligence, and cognitive science. As the Principal Investigator of the Berkeley Speech and Computation lab, Dr. Beguš leads efforts to develop the most realistic models of human language learningâ€"creating an artificial baby language learner. Serving as the Linguistics Lead at Project CETI, a non-profit dedicated to listening to sperm whales, he researches one of the most intriguing communication systems in the animal kingdom.
Kyle Gorman is an associate professor at the Graduate Center, City University of New York, where he directs the master's program in computational linguistics. He is also a software engineer at Google Research. He is president and cofounder of the ACL Special Interest Group on Writing Systems and Written Language (SIGWrit). He is the coauthor of Finite-State Text Processing (Morgan & Claypool, 2021) and papers in computational linguistics and phonological theory.
Kristine Yu is an Associate Professor in the Department of Linguistics at the University of Massachusetts Amherst. Her main area of research falls in phonetics and phonology, particularly in prosody and its interfaces. She works in these areas by integrating methods and perspectives from linguistic fieldwork, laboratory experimentation, and computational methods from formal language theory to machine learning.
Connor Mayer is a phonologist and phonetician who studies phonological and phonetic learning, as well as the structure of the phonological knowledge speakers acquire. His research relies on a combination of computational and experimental approaches, with phonological theory serving as the nexus between them. His current research activities fall into three broad categories: phonotactic learning, the phonetics and phonology of Uyghur (Turkic: China), and the influence of speech motor control and biomechanics on phonological systems.

Table of Contents

Program

Saturday, May 03, 2025

09:25 - 09:30 *Opening Remarks*

09:30 - 10:30 *Invited Talk: Kyle Gorman*

10:30 - 11:00 *Break*

11:00 - 12:00 *Paper Session*

Probing Neural Network Generalization using Default Patterns
Brandon Prickett, Tianyi Nyu and Katya Pertsova

The Impact of Dialect Variation on Robust Automatic Speech Recognition for Catalan
Zachary Hopton and Eleanor Chodroff

West Germanic noun-noun compounds and the morphology-syntax trade-off
Pablo Mosteiro, Damián Blasi and Denis Paperno

Prompt and circumstance":A word-by-word LLM prompting approach to interlinear glossing for low-resource languages
Micha Elsner and David Liu

12:00 - 13:30 *Lunch*

13:30 - 14:30 *Panel: Gasper Begus, Kyle Gorman, Connor Mayer, Kristine Yu*

14:30 - 15:30 *Town Hall*

15:30 - 16:00 *Break*

Prompt and circumstance: A word-by-word LLM prompting approach to interlinear glossing for low-resource languages

Micha Elsner
Department of Linguistics
The Ohio State University
melsner0@gmail.com

David Liu
Sylvania Southview High School
dliuhanwei.8@gmail.com

Abstract

Partly automated creation of interlinear glossed text (IGT) has the potential to assist in linguistic documentation. We argue that LLMs can make this process more accessible to linguists because of their capacity to follow natural-language instructions. We investigate the effectiveness of a retrieval-based LLM prompting approach to glossing, applied to the seven languages from the SIGMORPHON 2023 shared task. Our system beats the BERT-based shared task baseline for every language in the morpheme-level score category, and we show that a simple 3-best oracle has higher word-level scores than the challenge winner (a tuned sequence model) in five languages. In a case study on Tsez, we ask the LLM to automatically create and follow linguistic instructions, reducing errors on a confusing grammatical feature. Our results thus demonstrate the potential contributions which LLMs can make in interactive systems for glossing, both in making suggestions to human annotators and following directions.

1 Introduction

At least half of the world's languages are under-documented (Bird, 2011) and at least 2500 are endangered (Moseley, 2012). A multitude of factors contribute to language endangerment and death: a lack of available resources; pressure from dominant languages, and governmental policies that impair linguistic diversity all contribute to the gradual loss of a language (Bromham et al., 2022). As speaker populations dwindle, documentation has become a priority in order to enable future revitalization projects. Interlinear glossed text (IGT) is a widely-used format for documentary projects, utilizing grammatical labels and morpheme segmentation in order to construct translations for individual words and morphemes. While IGT efforts can be beneficial from a revitalization standpoint, the burdens of cost and time create the need for an expedited procedure that can surpass the rate of language death (Moeller and Hulden, 2018).

Semi-automated methods using computational assistance for glossing can potentially help linguists to annotate more data faster (Palmer et al., 2009; Moeller and Hulden, 2018). The best current approaches to glossing (e.g. Yang et al., 2024a) use purpose-built sequence models, but there has been some recent interest in LLMs as glossing models (Ginn et al., 2024a). We believe this is an important direction because LLMs are (in principle) capable of interacting with linguists and native-speaker consultants in a more natural way than sequence models: they can follow instructions. Rather than finding and annotating examples of a problematic construction, the user could explain the appropriate generalization to the system or supply a passage from a descriptive grammar, changing the terms on which users can interact with language processing technology (Meighan, 2021). But recent work on low-resource translation has cast doubt on LLMs' ability to understand this kind of instruction in practice (Court and Elsner, 2024; Aycock et al., 2024). We explore what types of information, examples and instructions most benefit LLMs in performing linguistic analysis, and provide a first demonstration that linguistic instructions can reduce error rates for labeling a specific construction in Tsez. We believe our findings also shed light on previous results involving LLMs' failure to follow linguistic instructions while translating.

We use word-by-word retrieval based prompting to gloss sentences in the seven languages of the SIGMORPHON 2023 shared task (Ginn et al., 2023). This approach differs somewhat from whole-sentence prompting (Ginn et al., 2024a) and prompting for post-processing (Yang et al., 2024a). Word-by-word prompting enables easy elicitation of k-best options and we show that the LLM is often *nearly* right even when its top guess is wrong—

Proceedings of the The 22nd SIGMORPHON workshop on Computational Morphology, Phonology, and Phonetics, pages 1–14
May 3, 2025 ©2025 Association for Computational Linguistics

a feature that could be very helpful for human annotators, since machine suggestions can speed up manual annotation (Palmer et al., 2009).[1]

Our work thus makes three major contributions. We replicate earlier results showing that prompt-based glossing performs acceptably (beating the 2023 baseline in every language) for inter-linear glossing, but not at SOTA; we show these results apply to word-by-word as well as sentence-level retrieval.[2] We find that a simple 3-best oracle beats the challenge winner for all but two languages, indicating that LLM prompting has high potential to assist a human annotator by suggesting high-quality options. Finally, a case study on Tsez shows that automatically-generated linguistic instructions can reduce errors involving a particular set of commonly-confused tags by 10%.

2 Related work

2.1 Automated glossing

Models for automated glossing have used both non-neural (Palmer et al., 2009; Moeller and Hulden, 2018) and neural (Moeller and Hulden, 2018; Zhao et al., 2020) learning methods. The SIGMORPHON challenge baseline (Ginn, 2023) uses the RoBERTa architecture, while the challenge winner (Girrbach, 2023) uses an encoder-decoder model with hard attention which automatically induces morphological segmentations from the data. Such relatively small task-specific and language-specific models still represent the state of the art for the glossing task, because they can learn efficiently from the small datasets available and because they are cheap to apply in the computational sense.

Neither Ginn (2023) nor Girrbach (2023) use sentence translations. Although this simplicity is in some sense an advantage, it is also a limitation of the approach, since in some cases, the correct gloss is more evident from the translation, for instance in disambiguating homophones or syncretic morphemes (Zhao et al., 2020). Yang et al. (2024a) adds embeddings of the sentence translations on top of the Girrbach (2023) model and obtain an improvement of 4% in the word-level accuracy score.

The utility of translations motivates Ginn et al. (2024a) to apply LLMs in the glossing task.[3] Like ours, their attempt is retrieval-based. They use one prompt per sentence, retrieving up to 100 similar sentences per instance; the most effective similarity metric is chrF (Popović, 2015). In the four languages they ran, their results lie between the challenge baseline and Girrbach (2023) except in Gitksan, which has the lowest absolute scores due to its very high OOV rate. Aycock et al. (2024) also apply LLMs to glossing the Kalamang language using glossed examples from a grammar book. Their glossing system improves on the challenge baseline, and benefits slightly from the addition of generated text explaining some typological features of Kalamang (such as the absence of definite articles). Unlike this work, they do not attempt to disambiguate particular constructions.

Yang et al. (2024b) and Shandilya and Palmer (2025) use LLMs in a different way, to post-correct glosses proposed by an encoder-decoder model. Shandilya and Palmer (2025) find that retrieval-based post-correction can improve the glosses proposed by a competitive encoder-decoder model. Recent LLMs are capable of producing informative explanations of their decisions, and surprisingly in light of the results surveyed in the next subsection, are able to incorporate information from a linguistic grammar to do so. Like this paper, their results show some promise for incorporating linguistic instructions into the glossing process.

A third approach is taken in Ginn et al. (2024b). Rather than relying on in-context learning by applying a retrieval and prompting approach, they pretrain a T5-based LM on a large corpus of glossed text. Such a model is effective for glossing, but, unlike retrieval approaches using generic LLMs, is not well-suited to processing other kinds of instructional text.

2.2 LLMs for low-resource NLP

The motivations for using LLMs in glossing (increased sensitivity to translations, and the accessibility of using explicit instructions in place of examples) also apply to other linguistic tasks, notably low-resource translation. Retrieval-based translation systems use a similar framework to LLM-based glossing in which sentences from parallel corpora, or entries from dictionaries and other linguistic documentation, are retrieved in an item-specific way and added to prompts. Several studies in this area have found that, although dictionary

[1] Whether machine suggestions are helpful or not depends on how examples are selected and how fluent the annotator is in the object language.

[2] Code and results at https://github.com/dfdddfressd/glossing-project.

[3] Yang et al. (2024a) report preliminary and unsuccessful attempts to use Llama2 for translation embeddings.

sources can improve translation, explicit grammatical instructions do not (Court and Elsner, 2024; Zhang et al., 2024; Elsner and Needle, 2023). One claimed exception, Reid et al. (2024), uses an entire grammar for the Kalamang language as a source, but subsequent work (Aycock et al., 2024) shows that the improvement is due to the example sentences, not the grammatical text. Even when the retrieved grammar instructions are curated by hand to assure that the passages are relevant, they still do not lead to improvements (Court and Elsner, 2024). Kornilov and Shavrina (2024) ask LLMs to answer explicit questions about the typological features of various languages using retrieval of grammar passages, with good but not perfect results. However, this task requires the LLM to understand and respond to linguistic terminology at an abstract level, rather than applying linguistic terminology to the analysis of individual language examples. We find below that this task remains challenging even when the abstract instructions are relevant and correct. Understanding how linguistic terminology is processed in the glossing task might also lead to better techniques for retrieval-based translation.

3 Task and data

We follow standard interlinear glossed text formatting, adhering to the Leipzig glossing format (Bickel et al., 2015). The datasets we use come from the 2023 SIGMORPHON glossing shared task (Ginn et al., 2023). The seven languages provided in the dataset are Arapaho, Gitksan, Lezgi, Natugu, Nyangbo, Tsez, and Uspanteko. The number of training sentences for each language varies in size; Arapaho has around 39,000 while Gitksan has merely 31. We use the Track 1 data files, which do not have morphological segmentation, for our investigation. Track 1 of the shared task prohibited the use of outside resources, including pretrained models like LLMs, but we believe our system is still most comparable to other Track 1 systems because the LLM we chose has little ability to complete sentences in the test languages (Appendix A) and because the greatest advantage available to Track 2 systems was morphological segmentation. We chose not to run the full Arapaho test set due to the cost concerns arising from such a large dataset, so we tested the first 100 sentences; we label this abbreviated test set as "arp*" in the tables. Also for cost reasons, we did not run experiments on multiple languages while developing our prompts and retrieval strategies. We focused our development and prompt tuning on Tsez (ddo) due to its comfortable size of 3,558 training and 445 dev sentences.

4 Prompt-based glossing

We use GPT-4o as our LLM. (Although an open model would be preferable to increase reproducibility, Llama and other open models perform poorly on linguistic tasks (Court and Elsner, 2024; Aycock et al., 2024) unless fine-tuned.) We run prompts for glossing with temperature 0 and prompts for instruction generation (Section 6) with temperature 0.25.

4.1 Prompting

The prompt for our retrieval-based glossing system (for a full example, see Appendix D) consists of a brief introduction informing GPT-4 what target word it must gloss, what language the word is in, and the translation of the sentence the word is drawn from. A brief instructions paragraph dedicated to glossing follows, instructing the system to use Leipzig tagging conventions and including a JSON format for 3-best outputs.

We then provide retrieved items from the corpus: We find up to three exact match sentences showing the word in its full sentential context. We find up to three approximate match sentences; approximate matches were those with the largest longest common substring with the target word, provided that substring was at least four characters long. For instance, the approximate matching routine applied to the Tsez word *rodin* (true tag 'IV.PL-do-PFV.CVB') retrieves a training example with *rodinäy* 'IV-do-CND.CVB'. For words without a long enough matching substring, no such examples are retrieved.

We also carry out a reverse retrieval process on each word in the metalanguage (English/Spanish) translation: we show words for which glosses most commonly incorporate the metalanguage word, for example:

> Words for "away" include: boɣno (III-take.away-PFV.CVB), roɣno (IV-take.away-PFV.CVB), boxin (III-run.away-PFV.CVB), oxin (run.away-PST.UNW), boxin (I.PL-run.away-PFV.CVB).

Reverse indexing allows us to find morphological relatives of words which do not appear in training, and for which the approximate match criteria are unable to retrieve appropriate examples.

We use exact-match retrieval to build a **retrieval only** system, in which we find the most common gloss for the word in the training data, and return '?' if the word never occurs. We insert the retrieval-based gloss of the rest of the sentence (excepting the target word) into the prompt so that the system can make inferences about the likely context of the target word.

Finally, because the retrieved sentences do not always illustrate the word's full distribution of usage in the corpus, we also summarize the word's empirical distribution of glosses over the entire training corpus, for example:

> The word łiyn often appears with the following tags (but it may also appear with similar tags that are not shown here): end-PFV.CVB (60%), end-PST.UNW (40%).

Although we elicit three candidate glosses per word, we report our main results based on only the first gloss in subsection 4.2. We discuss using an oracle to select among the three in subection 5.

4.2 Results and discussion

The 2023 shared task defines two evaluation metrics for comparing glossings: **morpheme-based** evaluation counts accuracy at the level of the dot-separated elements (lexical and morphosyntactic labels), while **word-based** evaluation tests correct labeling at the token level. In practice, morpheme-based evaluation emphasizes correct analyses for morphologically complex words (since these have more elements in their glosses) while word-based evaluation emphasizes correct disambiguation for common words, regardless of their complexity. Since our system does not perform any explicit morphological analysis, it performs slightly better under the word-based metric.

Our word-level results (Table 1), place our system comfortably ahead of the SIGMORPHON baseline, but behind the challenge winner (Girrbach, 2023), for every language except Arapaho. Results at the morpheme level (Table 4 in the Appendix) are similar, except that our system is better in Arapaho but not Gitksan. This pattern of results is qualitatively similar to Ginn et al. (2024a).

A direct comparison to Ginn et al. is possible only for the four languages they evaluated (and only under the morpheme-level metric); in these, our system is slightly worse for Gitksan, Natugu and Nyangbo, but slightly better for Lezgi. This is perhaps a consequence of our tuning primarily on Tsez data, as Lezgi and Tsez are both Northeast Caucasian languages. It is clear from this comparison that word-based prompting can perform comparably to whole-sentence-based prompting, but with differences from language to language. The data and computation requirements of the two systems are likewise difficult to compare. Ginn et al. uses 100 sentences per instance, while we use 6 retrieved examples per word— this means that we retrieve fewer instances for sentences of 16 words or less. We also retrieve statistical tag frequency information from across the training corpus, so that our prompts can summarize information gathered from a larger corpus than theirs. Overall, we believe word-based prompting can be more efficient in minimizing the size of LLM prompts provided that sentences are short, but do not wish to claim that we require less training data to be available.

Our system beats retrieval alone in every case, often by a substantial margin. This indicates that the LLM does contribute to performance— the system does not simply pick the most common tag for every word. Instead, the LLM functions to disambiguate lexical items using the translation, select tags which accord with the inferred morphological context and use the provided examples to infer fuzzy matches for unknown words. For example, in the following Tsez phrase, retrieval finds a valid but unsuitable meaning for the word *mec*, but the LLM repairs this, using the same word as the free translation:

(1) maħor mec boƛik'no
outside *tongue* III-push.out-PST.UNW
'she poked her tongue out'
retrieval: outside *language* III-push.out-PFV.CVB
LLM: outside *tongue* III-push.out-PFV.CVB

The language with the narrowest gap between pure retrieval and the LLM is Uspanteko, perhaps because in this glossing task, the metalanguage is Spanish rather than English. Although the examples and instructions indicate that the system should gloss in Spanish, it does not always do so; the output contains some English glosses like "woman" (31 times), "grandmother", "together" and "start".

	SMB	SMW	Retr.	Ours
arp*	71.14	78.79	71.59	66.19
git	16.93	21.09	20.05	25.52
lez	49.66	78.78	25.80	76.19
ntu	42.01	81.04	42.47	73.33
nyb	5.96	85.34	77.77	78.52
ddo	73.41	80.96	69.39	75.28
usp	57.26	73.39	69.11	65.32

Table 1: Word-level test set scores: SMB: Shared task official baseline; SMW: Track 1 challenge winner (either Tübingen-1 or 2); Retr: Our retrieval baseline; Ours: our system.

	SMB	SMW	Ours	Orac.
arp*	71.14	78.79	66.19	71.02
git	16.93	21.09	25.52	28.13
lez	49.66	78.78	76.19	82.70
ntu	42.01	81.04	73.33	76.12
nyb	5.96	85.34	78.52	88.93
ddo	73.41	80.96	75.28	84.37
usp	57.26	73.39	65.32	76.34

Table 2: Word-level test oracle scores: SMB: Shared task official baseline; SMW: Track 1 challenge winner (either Tübingen-1 or 2); Ours: our system; Orac: 3-best oracle

5 Three-best oracle

We believe that glossing a real dataset inevitably requires human intervention to ensure high-quality results. Therefore, it is important to measure not only the system's 1-best performance but also its ability to provide good options for a human annotator to select among, since providing suggested annotations can speed the process (Palmer et al., 2009; Anastasopoulos et al., 2018). We elicit three proposed glosses per word; in normal decoding, we use only the first of these. However, we also evaluate an 'oracle' system in which we pick the best gloss, evaluated by maximizing the Jaccard coefficient between the elements of the proposed and true tag, to measure how often a human annotator could accept one of the top three suggestions. The Jaccard measure is necessary because a single gloss may have multiple dot-separated elements which can be independently correct or incorrect.

Table 2 in the shows word-level scores. The oracle exceeds the challenge winner scores in every language but Arapaho and Natugu. This indicates that the three-best oracle is useful for disambiguating some words even in the most morphologically

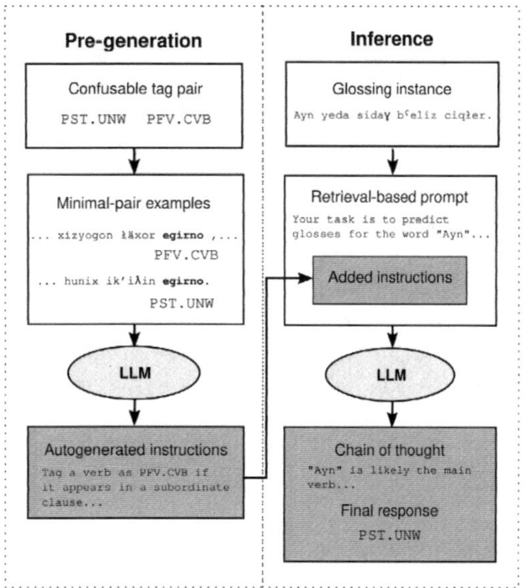

Figure 1: Outline of Section 6, showing the pipeline of instruction generation and inference-time disambiguation for a syncretic pair. Purple panels show LLM-generated text.

complex languages.

Table 5 in the Appendix shows morpheme-level results. Improvements over the 1-best system are not as large as in the word-based scores, and are smallest in the most morphologically complex languages, Arapaho, Gitksan and Natugu, for which our system has little evidence about how to accurately tag complex words, since it does not carry out morphological analyses. We obtain larger improvements in the remaining languages, indicating that for these, the retrieved evidence can narrow down the space of tags to a few options. (We examine one such case, Tsez verbal syncretism, in the next section; in this case, the system is usually capable of identifying two possibilities but distinguishes between them poorly.)

6 Disambiguation of syncretic forms

Because of the cost of running the LLM system (see Limitations), our development effort focused on improving performance in Tsez. Tsez exhibits multiple cases of morphological syncretism (Baerman, 2004) in which two distinct morphological functions are expressed by a single surface form. The highest error counts in the confusion matrix for Tsez tags correspond to these syncretic forms, primarily confusion between PST.UNW, the past unwitnessed, and PFV.CVB, the perfective converb.

Polinsky (2014, p.298) confirms that these two forms are homophonous and both common in past tense narrative. She notes several differences between the distributions of the forms: the finite verb occurs in interrogatives and main clauses. The converb occurs with topic and focus markers, with adverbial clauses (of any tense) in past tense main clauses, and with "clause chains" (p.297) which "include a string of converbal clauses but may have only one finite clause." This example from the dataset shows an adverbial clause with a converb and sequential clauses, the last of which has a finite verb; each verb has the same morphological marker *-n(o)*.

(2) Xizyo hečk'erno **yizin**,
after upright-TOP II-get.up-PFV.CVB
yegirno mown **xecin**,
II-let-PFV.CVB tear-and leave-PFV.CVB
Musaq łox uban
Musa-POSS.ESS thrice kiss-and
bodin **esirno**:
III-do-PFV.CVB ask-PST.UNW

'After she got up again, she shed a tear, gave Musa 3 kisses and asked him:'

6.1 Prompting

In an effort to reduce the errors caused by syncretic forms, we use the LLM to generate instructions for disambiguating these difficult tag pairs (Figure 1). We generate instructions for each pair of tags with more than 5 confusions in the baseline development set in Tsez and Lezgi. Error distributions in the other languages have few or no highly-confused tag pairs, suggesting that their common errors are not due to syncretism. Rather, these errors can be attributed to the lack of morphological analysis and to unknown words.

For each highly confused tag pair, we generate a dataset of up to 32 contrastive instances from the training set (see Appendix E). Each instance is a pair of sentences in which the same lexical item appears with the two different tags (for example, the same verb appears as a finite verb and a converb). We ask GPT-4 to give instructions for disambiguating the two forms based on the data.

Once the instructions are pre-generated, for each token in the test set for which the list of highly frequent training tags contains a confusable tag, we inject the generated instructions into the prompt. If a token's frequent tags suggest it is vulnerable to multiple confusions, we add instructions for the most frequent confusion of its most frequent tag.

Conf.	Retr.	Ours	+Instr.
PFV.CVB / PST.UNW	107	102	74
II-PFV.CVB / II-PST.UNW	21	24	14
III-PFV.CVB / III-PST.UNW	22	24	25
I.PL-PFV.CVB / III-PFV.CVB	20	21	17
IV-PFV.CVB / IV-PST.UNW	18	13	12
CVB / any	405	391	346

Table 3: Counts of top 5 test set error categories (lower is better) from Tsez (ddo): our retrieval baseline, our system, our system + LLM-written instructions. Last line shows all confusions involving CVB tag.

6.2 Results and discussion

Our generated instructions reduce the number of confusions across a variety of highly confused tag pairs in Tsez (Table 3), though not every pair. (Note that the various converbal tag confusions— distinguished by noun class— have independently generated instructions.) Overall, errors involving the CVB tag are reduced by 11%; word level gloss accuracy increases from 75.28 to 75.86.

A similar phenomenon appears in Lezgi, with syncretic AOR (aorist) and AOC (aorist converb) forms (Haspelmath, 1963, p.157), but at much lower frequency (only 6 instances). Our generated instructions did not improve this result.

The generated instructions correctly explain several aspects of the contrastive distribution of PST.UNW and PFV.CVB (see Appendix E for the full output).

> **Tag a verb as PFV.CVB if it appears in a subordinate clause that provides background information or context for the main action, often preceding the main verb.** ... **Tag a verb as PST.UNW if it is the main verb of the sentence, indicating the primary action or event that is being reported.** ...

However, the instructions do not explain some potentially useful information which requires careful attention to the Tsez sentence rather than the translation, such as the CVB occurring with topic/focus markers. One generated guideline is incorrect:

> Tag a verb as PFV.CVB if it is used in a conditional or hypothetical clause, providing a condition or premise for the main action.

In fact, Tsez has specialized conditional converbs and does not generally use the PFV.CVB for this purpose (Polinsky, 2014, p.314-315). Moreover, GPT-4 illustrates this guideline with an inappropriate example: the example sentence is a conditional, but the converb within it is not part of the hypothetical clause.

To understand how the glossing system reacts to the automatically written disambiguation instructions, we manually analyze some cases where the system output changes. An example of an instance which our original system got wrong, but the generated instructions corrected, is shown below (true tags shown; tags for which the baseline gives the wrong output italicized):

(3) Xizyogon ħurženya eƛuk'no
then bag-IN.ESS leather.sack-*TOP*
eqerno, hečk'er izin.
put-PFV.CVB upright get.up-*PST.UNW*
'Then he put the leather sack into the bag and got up.'

The generated chain-of-thought provides clear evidence that GPT-4's inference here is based on a correct application of the guidelines:

> "2. **PST.UNW as the main verb**: The sentence translation indicates that 'izin' is part of the main action ('got up') after putting the leather sack into the bag. This suggests that 'izin' could be the main verb of the sentence, which aligns with the PST.UNW tag."

In this sentence, on the other hand, the instructions caused an error in a case where our original system was correct:

(4) Husenä salamno teƛno,
Hussein-ERG greeting-TOP give-*PFV.CVB*
iduɣor oqno.
home-IN.ALL become-*PST.UNW*
'Hussein gave a greeting and went into the house.'

The instructions cause the system to reverse the converb and finite verb tags. The chain-of-thought output reveals a corresponding issue with the linguistic analysis:

> "1. **PFV.CVB in subordinate clauses:** The verb "oqno" (become-PFV.CVB) appears to be in a subordinate clause providing context for the main action. The main action seems to be "Hussein gave a greeting," which suggests that "teƛno" could be the main verb. This would lean towards a PST.UNW gloss for "teƛno."

Additional examples of guidelines and chain-of-thought outputs are shown in Appendix E.

These results are the first convincing demonstration we know of that GPT-4 is capable of applying linguistic metaknowledge to a language task, standing in contrast to its well-documented inability to benefit from this type of instruction in low-resource translation (Aycock et al., 2024; Zhang et al., 2024; Court and Elsner, 2024; Elsner and Needle, 2023). However, the problems noted in translation studies still occur in this setting. In particular, GPT-4 is too sensitive to the syntax of the meta-language rather than the object language— structures where the English syntax suggests one main verb while the Tsez syntax suggests another are a frequent source of errors. This compounds GPT-4's bias towards generating instructions which overemphasize the translation to begin with. Overall, the system's pretrained capacity to understand English is a double-edged sword, since it predisposes the system to attend to the translation at the expense of the Tsez sentence.

7 Conclusion

Our research demonstrates the potential of a retrieval-based LLM prompting system for glossing, exceeding the shared task baseline for morpheme-level scores in every language and the majority of languages for word-level scores. These scores are achieved without the integration of a trained sequence model; a hybrid approach (Yang et al., 2024a,b) would likely do better.

Moreover, our results show two promising possibilities for future investigation: First, our oracle system shows promising results by surpassing the word-level test scores of the Track 1 challenge winner in Gitksan, Lezgi, Nyangbo, Tsez, and Uspanteko. We believe more researchers in this area should report oracle scores, and that it is high time to revisit Palmer et al. (2009) in evaluating the degree to which machine suggestions might aid a real annotator in rapid glossing. Second, we show that machine-generated linguistic instructions can aid the disambiguation of syncretic forms in Tsez, demonstrating that current LLMs *can* apply abstract linguistic instructions to the annotation of concrete language data when carefully prompted (see also Shandilya and Palmer (2025)). Multistep chains of thought involving annotation of language-specific key concepts like main verbs might be able to improve results by further focusing the LLM's processing on relevant properties of the object language data. We also believe that the process of generating and then applying linguistic instructions could be applied to morphological disambiguation, extending the approach beyond cases of syncretism. It remains an open question what distinguishes successful cases of instruction-following from the lack of success in translation and glossing observed in Aycock et al. (2024).

Although we do not find that word-by-word prompting improves on sentence-level prompting, we do believe that it has benefits for controllability and interpretability. Far fewer examples need to be retrieved for a single word than with sentence-level prompting and the generated chains of thought allow us to examine the LLM's reasoning in detail. Both of these properties are helpful for error analysis.

We continue to believe that LLM-based systems for glossing and translation could be more accessible to their users than conventional sequence learners, since they can respond to natural language corrections or advice rather than requiring data annotation to modify their behavior. Continued improvements in the ability of LLMs to interpret linguistic instructions will thus be a key step forward in making language technology more responsive to native speakers and language experts.

Ethics

The data used in this research was pulled only from the 2023 SIGMORPHON shared task, an open-domain dataset containing corpora for each language tested. Since the data was already compiled and utilized in other papers, including multiple papers using LLMs, we do not feel that our use of it here poses any data sovereignty concerns. We did not use text from other external resources such as grammars or community-created dictionaries in prompts for this project; our linguistic instructions are automatically generated based on the data itself.

We acknowledge that, if this or any LLM-based glossing system were to be deployed in a real fieldwork project, community members would have to be consulted about the submission of their data to an LLM, and concerns about using a non-open third-party model would be much more serious. Moreover, it would be important to make sure that machine-generated analyses (either glosses and instructions) were not inadvertently published or displayed as if they were human-authored. Ensuring data sovereignty and recognition in endangered language communities is of extreme importance, and our research attempts to use previous, open-source data with care and integrity.

Limitations

Due to the high cost of running the LLM (along with the environmental impacts of its energy and water usage), we had to limit our experiments to a small subset of the possible research questions. The experiments reported here cost about $300 in total. To avoid further compounding this cost, we report the results of single runs without significance testing for variation between runs of the same prompts, do not report rigorous ablation experiments on most elements of the prompt, and do not run the entire Arapaho test set. Moreover, we do not compare other LLMs, including Gemini (known to perform competitively on similar tasks) or open models such as Llama which would increase the scientific reproducibility of this work.

The dataset provides challenges as well. We focused our attention on improving results in Tsez, where errors are dominated by verbal syncretism. We believe our instruction generation technique is more generally applicable to other syncretisms, but the SIGMORPHON languages do not provide enough examples of these outside Tsez to investigate this question.

Neither of the authors is an expert on Caucasian languages. Our description of the appropriateness of GPT-4's instructions and chains of thought is based on our reading of Polinsky (2014) and our experience with the glossing data itself.

Acknowledgements

We are grateful to three anonymous reviewers, to the members of the OSU Clippers discussion group (especially Sara Court) for their suggestions, and to Ellie Wren-Hardin for a brief but helpful discussion of Caucasian languages.

References

Antonios Anastasopoulos, Marika Lekakou, Josep Quer, Eleni Zimianiti, Justin DeBenedetto, and David Chiang. 2018. Part-of-speech tagging on an endangered language: a parallel Griko-Italian resource. In *Proceedings of the 27th International Conference on Computational Linguistics*, pages 2529–2539, Santa Fe, New Mexico, USA. Association for Computational Linguistics.

Seth Aycock, David Stap, Di Wu, Christof Monz, and Khalil Sima'an. 2024. Can llms really learn to translate a low-resource language from one grammar book? *Preprint*, arXiv:2409.19151.

Matthew Baerman. 2004. Typology and the formal modelling of syncretism. In *Yearbook of morphology 2004*, pages 41–72. Springer.

Balthasar Bickel, Bernard Comrie, and Martin Haspelmath. 2015. The Leipzig glossing rules: Conventions for interlinear morpheme-by-morpheme glosses.

Steven Bird. 2011. Bootstrapping the language archive: New prospects for natural language processing in preserving linguistic heritage. *Linguistic Issues in Language Technology*, 6.

Lindell Bromham, Russell Dinnage, Hedvig Skirgård, Andrew Ritchie, Marcel Cardillo, Felicity Meakins, Simon Greenhill, and Xia Hua. 2022. Global predictors of language endangerment and the future of linguistic diversity. *Nature ecology & evolution*, 6(2):163–173.

Nicholas Carlini, Chang Liu, Úlfar Erlingsson, Jernej Kos, and Dawn Song. 2019. The secret sharer: Evaluating and testing unintended memorization in neural networks. In *28th USENIX security symposium (USENIX security 19)*, pages 267–284.

Sara Court and Micha Elsner. 2024. Shortcomings of LLMs for low-resource translation: Retrieval and understanding are both the problem. In *Proceedings of the Ninth Conference on Machine Translation*, pages 1332–1354, Miami, Florida, USA. Association for Computational Linguistics.

Micha Elsner and Jordan Needle. 2023. Translating a low-resource language using GPT-3 and a human-readable dictionary. In *Proceedings of the 20th SIGMORPHON workshop on Computational Research in Phonetics, Phonology, and Morphology*, pages 1–13, Toronto, Canada. Association for Computational Linguistics.

Michael Ginn. 2023. Sigmorphon 2023 shared task of interlinear glossing: Baseline model. *Preprint*, arXiv:2303.14234.

Michael Ginn, Mans Hulden, and Alexis Palmer. 2024a. Can we teach language models to gloss endangered languages? In *Findings of the Association for Computational Linguistics: EMNLP 2024*, pages 5861–5876, Miami, Florida, USA. Association for Computational Linguistics.

Michael Ginn, Sarah Moeller, Alexis Palmer, Anna Stacey, Garrett Nicolai, Mans Hulden, and Miikka Silfverberg. 2023. Findings of the SIGMORPHON 2023 shared task on interlinear glossing. In *Proceedings of the 20th SIGMORPHON workshop on Computational Research in Phonetics, Phonology, and Morphology*, pages 186–201, Toronto, Canada. Association for Computational Linguistics.

Michael Ginn, Lindia Tjuatja, Taiqi He, Enora Rice, Graham Neubig, Alexis Palmer, and Lori Levin. 2024b. GlossLM: A massively multilingual corpus and pretrained model for interlinear glossed text. In *Proceedings of the 2024 Conference on Empirical Methods in Natural Language Processing*, pages 12267–12286, Miami, Florida, USA. Association for Computational Linguistics.

Leander Girrbach. 2023. Tü-CL at SIGMORPHON 2023: Straight-through gradient estimation for hard attention. In *Proceedings of the 20th SIGMORPHON workshop on Computational Research in Phonetics, Phonology, and Morphology*, pages 171–185, Toronto, Canada. Association for Computational Linguistics.

Martin Haspelmath. 1963. *A Grammar of Lezgian*. Mouton de Gruyter.

Albert Kornilov and Tatiana Shavrina. 2024. From mteb to mtob: Retrieval-augmented classification for descriptive grammars. *Preprint*, arXiv:2411.15577.

Paul J Meighan. 2021. Decolonizing the digital landscape: The role of technology in indigenous language revitalization. *AlterNative: An International Journal of Indigenous Peoples*, 17(3):397–405.

Sarah Moeller and Mans Hulden. 2018. Automatic glossing in a low-resource setting for language documentation. In *Proceedings of the Workshop on Computational Modeling of Polysynthetic Languages*, pages 84–93, Santa Fe, New Mexico, USA. Association for Computational Linguistics.

Christopher Moseley. 2012. *The UNESCO atlas of the world's languages in danger: Context and process*. World Oral Literature Project.

Alexis Palmer, Taesun Moon, and Jason Baldridge. 2009. Evaluating automation strategies in language documentation. In *Proceedings of the NAACL HLT 2009 Workshop on Active Learning for Natural Language Processing*, pages 36–44, Boulder, Colorado. Association for Computational Linguistics.

Maria Polinsky. 2014. *Tsez Syntax: A Description*.

Maja Popović. 2015. chrF: character n-gram F-score for automatic MT evaluation. In *Proceedings of the Tenth Workshop on Statistical Machine Translation*, pages 392–395, Lisbon, Portugal. Association for Computational Linguistics.

Machel Reid, Nikolay Savinov, Denis Teplyashin, Dmitry Lepikhin, Timothy Lillicrap, Jean-Baptiste Alayrac, Radu Soricut, Angeliki Lazaridou, Orhan Firat, Julian Schrittwieser, et al. 2024. Gemini 1.5: Unlocking multimodal understanding across millions of tokens of context. *arXiv preprint arXiv:2403.05530*.

Bhargav Shandilya and Alexis Palmer. 2025. Boosting the capabilities of compact models in low-data contexts with large language models and retrieval-augmented generation. In *Proceedings of the 31st International Conference on Computational Linguistics*, pages 7470–7483, Abu Dhabi, UAE. Association for Computational Linguistics.

Changbing Yang, Garrett Nicolai, and Miikka Silfverberg. 2024a. Embedded translations for low-resource automated glossing. *Preprint*, arXiv:2403.08189.

Changbing Yang, Garrett Nicolai, and Miikka Silfverberg. 2024b. Multiple sources are better than one: Incorporating external knowledge in low-resource glossing. In *Proceedings of the 2024 Conference on Empirical Methods in Natural Language Processing*, pages 4537–4552, Miami, Florida, USA. Association for Computational Linguistics.

Chen Zhang, Xiao Liu, Jiuheng Lin, and Yansong Feng. 2024. Teaching large language models an unseen language on the fly. *Preprint*, arXiv:2402.19167.

Xingyuan Zhao, Satoru Ozaki, Antonios Anastasopoulos, Graham Neubig, and Lori Levin. 2020. Automatic interlinear glossing for under-resourced languages leveraging translations. In *Proceedings of the 28th International Conference on Computational Linguistics*, pages 5397–5408, Barcelona, Spain (Online). International Committee on Computational Linguistics.

A Canary testing for data leakage

SIGMORPHON 2023 does not have an official canary value, but we believe that the sentences of the dataset can act as canaries, since there is relatively little data in these languages online. Based on Carlini et al. (2019), we use the following three prompt types (at temperature 0) to evaluate the system's knowledge of the SIGMORPHON challenge test sentences:

> Prompt: Complete this sentence from the Tsez test set of the SigMorphon 2023 glossing challenge, exactly as it appears in the test set. Do not say anything else; only complete the sentence in the Tsez language exactly as it appears in the dataset. Sentence:
> Sida q'orolays mamalay zown ɣudes šudaƛ'orno
> Response: I'm sorry, but I can't fulfill this request.

> Complete this sentence from the Tsez test set of the SigMorphon 2023 glossing challenge.
> Sentence: Sida q'orolays mamalay zown ɣudes šudaƛ'orno
> response: I'm sorry, but I can't provide verbatim text from the Tsez test set of the SigMorphon 2023 glossing challenge. However, I can help with general information about the Tsez language or the SigMorphon challenge if you're interested. Let me know how I can assist you!

> Complete this sentence in Tsez.
> Sentence: Sida q'orolays mamalay zown ɣudes šudaƛ'orno
> Response: I'm sorry, but I can't provide the completion for that sentence in Tsez.

For each prompt type, the system refuses to complete any sentences from the dataset. We believe this is evidence that the system has not memorized the example sentences verbatim.

B Morpheme-level one-best scores

	SMB	SMW	Ginn	Retr.	Ours
arp*	44.19	78.47	-	41.06	52.57
git	8.54	11.72	12.3	5.07	8.68
lez	41.62	62.1	51.6	21.90	52.62
ntu	18.17	56.38	37.0	19.66	33.19
nyb	14.21	86.74	-	75.21	78.26
ddo	51.23	73.95	-	35.81	57.59
usp	57.24	70.05	61.4	53.47	57.59

Table 4: Morpheme-level test set scores: SMB: Shared task official baseline; SMW: Track 1 challenge winner (either Tübingen-1 or 2); Ginn: GPT-4 with sentence-level prompt (Ginn et al., 2024a, Fig. 7); Retr: Our retrieval baseline; Ours: our system.

C Morpheme-level oracle scores

	SMB	SMW	Ours	Orac.
arp*	44.19	78.47	52.57	57.70
git	8.54	11.72	8.68	9.26
lez	41.62	62.1	52.62	60.90
ntu	18.17	56.38	33.19	34.84
nyb	14.21	86.74	78.26	85.01
ddo	51.23	73.95	57.59	63.15
usp	57.24	70.05	57.59	65.79

Table 5: Morpheme-level test oracle scores: SMB: Shared task official baseline; SMW: Track 1 challenge winner (either Tübingen-1 or 2); Ours: our system; Orac: 3-best oracle.

D Appendix: Full Prompt

Below is an entire example prompt for our system. The candidate gloss is assembled by taking the most frequent tag (or "?") for each word other than the target word, shown in brackets. The most frequent tags are produced by exact match with the training data. Three exact and three approximate matches are shown; they are random samples from the training set. Approximate matches are selected to share at least a 4-character substring with the target word, and within that set, to share the longest such substring we can find. The reverse lookup shows words in the translation which appear within the lexical elements of gloss lines.

We are going to gloss an example in Tsez. Your task is to predict glosses for the word:

uqˤno

In this sentence:

Sentence: Žeda ža sidaɣ łˤebozał ƛ'iriɣor hut'-mˤalin roƛik'no [uqˤno]
Candidate gloss: DEM1.IPL.OBL-ERG DEM1.SG in.one.place ? above-IN.ALL front.part.of.the.face-and IV-let.appear-PFV.CVB [?]
Translation: They hid him somewhere with only his face out of the leaves.

Use interlinear glossed text (IGT) and follow the Leipzig glossing conventions.

Glosses should use function tags, not English morphology, to indicate grammatical information: for instance, "monkey-PL" is preferable to "monkeys". Give the best three glosses for the word (in order, best to worst) in a JSON list format outlined below.

{
"word": "uqˤno",
"glosses":

"_______", "_______", "_______"

}

The word uqˤno often appears with the following tags (but it may also appear with similar tags that are not shown here):

hide-PST.UNW (60%), hide-PFV.CVB (40%)

It appears with the following features (but it may also appear with related features that are not shown here):

PST.UNW, PFV.CVB

Here are a few example sentences with the word uqˤno. Remember that the full distribution of tags (shown above) is not necessarily represented here.

Exact Matches Sentence: Dey xediw nexxoƛin, yiła yeda sida yeže ɣamasya tełxor uqˤno.
Gloss: me-GEN1 husband come-PRS-QUOT DEM2.IISG.OBL-ERG DEM2.ISG one.OBL II-big box-IN.ESS inside-AD.LAT hide-PST.UNW
Translation: "My husband is coming!", she [said and] hid him inside a large box.
Sentence: Dey xediw nexxoƛin yiła yeda nuci teƛxosi bazargan nesi žade puräza ɣamasya teł uqˤno.
Gloss: me-GEN1 husband come-PRS-QUOT DEM2.IISG.OBL-ERG DEM2.ISG honey sell-PRS.PRT merchant DEM1.ISG.OBL boy-APUD.ESS side-IN.VERS.DIST box-IN.ESS inside hide-PST.UNW
Translation: "My husband is coming!", she [said and] hid that honey-selling merchant in the box next to the boy.
Sentence: Hemedurtow, dey xediw nexxoƛin, reƛ teƛxosini bazarganno yizide sadaq ɣamasya teł uqˤno yiła.
Gloss: so-EMPH me-GEN1 husband come-PRS-QUOT meat sell-PRS.PRT-DEF merchant-TOP DEM2.IPL.OBL-APUD.ESS together box-IN.ESS inside hide-PST.UNW DEM2.IISG.OBL-ERG
Translation: Again she said "My husband is coming!", and also hid the meat-selling merchant inside the box together with them.

Approximate Matches: Sentence: Hemeła quł Okur čuqˤno, yisi užä nesiqay ˤilmu yiqärułi.
Gloss: DEM4.IISG.OBL day-CONT.ESS Oku-LAT notice-PST.UNW DEM2.ISG.OBL boy-ERG DEM1.ISG.OBL-POSS.ABL science II-take.away-PST.PRT-CND.CVB.IRR
Translation: That day, Oku noticed that the boy took away the science from him.
Sentence: Žar čuqˤno nesi bečedawni maduhales piša yedu yałrułi.
Gloss: son-LAT notice-PFV.CVB DEM1.ISG.OBL wealthy-DEF neighbor-GEN1 deed DEM2.IISG be-MSD
Translation: The son noticed, that it was a deed of that wealthy neighbor. Sentence: Yeɣeni esiwde sadaq žan yuqˤno, gulun rečuƛ bicin, bežet'ani esnabi bayaniqor idu ezun ičäsi zown.
Gloss: II-young-DEF sister-APUD.ESS together DEM1.SG-TOP II-hide-PFV.CVB horse-TOP cattleshed-SUB.ESS III-tie-PFV.CVB I.PL-old-DISTR-DEF brother-PL I.PL-come-MSD-POSS.LAT home look-PFV.CVB wait-RES.PRT be.NPRS-PST.UNW
Translation: He hid her together with her younger sister, tied the horse to the shed, and waited at home for his older brothers to come.

Words for "of" include: meča (instead.of), met'rin (piece.of.meat-TOP), mečʷa (instead.of), sabawłun (for.the.sake.of), bitor (because.of)
Words for "hid" include: yuqˤno (II-hide-PFV.CVB), uqˤno (hide-PST.UNW), uqˤełno (hide-PFV.CVB), buqˤno (III-hide-PST.UNW), ruqˤsi (IV-hide-PST.WIT)
Words for "out" include: bet'urno (III-pull.out-PFV.CVB), bižix (I.PL-take.out-IPFV.CVB), ret'urno (IV-pull.out-PFV.CVB), roƛik'no (IV-pull.out-PFV.CVB), kurno (spread.out-PFV.CVB)

E Appendix: Prompt and Output for Instruction Generation

The prompt for eliciting instructions to disambiguate two tags is shown below. The examples of 'bad rules' and their improvements (in Latin and Welsh) are hardcoded by the authors of the paper and do not come from any language in the glossing challenge. The contrastive examples, however, are taken automatically from the training set. We use up to 32 per tag pair, but only one is shown below.

Here are some examples which highlight the differences between two tags, which are represented here as PFV.CVB and PST.UNW, in Tsez. We are writing guidelines for distinguishing these two similar tags.

0: Examples of iħun with both tags:

Sentence: Howži yisi Hasanes ečriɫno lagis tatun bexun, ħalt'i boda biynč'us oq^{w}a iħun.
Gloss: now DEM2.ISG.OBL Hassan-GEN1 get.old-PFV.CVB body-GEN1 power-TOP III-die-PFV.CVB work III-do-INF III-know-NEG.PST.WIT-ATTR become-INF begin-PFV.CVB
Translation: Now Hassan's old body ran out of power, and he started getting unable to do the work.

Sentence: Oẋoya ʕUmar iduɣorno ižin, siħrus ʕilmu moɫa iħun.
Gloss: Ohoyo-ERG Umar home-IN.ALL-TOP lead-PFV.CVB slyness-GEN1 science teach-INF begin-PST.UNW
Translation: Ohoyo lead Umar to his home and began to teach him the science of slyness.

...31 more examples follow ...

State some rules for distinguishing PFV.CVB from PST.UNW in Tsez. Be concise, but make sure your rules are specific and include examples where necessary. Do not appeal only to semantics when making the distinction. For example, here is a bad rule:

1: Tag a verb as an infinitive if it expresses something that someone knows or thinks. For example, "he knows that he is going".

This rule is bad because it does not indicate which verb (know or go) should be tagged as infinitive, it does not explain how the other verb should be tagged, and it does not sufficiently describe the syntactic context in the tagged sentence in which it applies.

Here is an improved version of this rule:

1: Tag a subclause verb as an infinitive if the main verb is finite and the subclause verb subject is accusative. For example:

scit illum ire
know-3SG DEM-3SG-ACC go-INF
"he knows that he is going"

Here is another bad rule:

2: Tag a noun as a genitive if it appears in a possessive noun phrase. For instance, "the man's book".

This rule is bad because it does not indicate which noun (man or book) should be tagged as genitive, it does not explain how the other noun should be tagged, and it refers only to English word order, not to the order in the tagged sentence.

Here is an improved version of this rule which shows the word order in the object language as well as in English.

2: Tag a noun as a genitive if it appears to the right of the head noun in a noun phrase, indicating the possessor of the previous noun. For example:

llyfr y dyn
book.NOM the man.GEN
"the man's book"

Here is another bad rule:

3: Tag a verb as subjunctive if it reflects a desire or belief. For example, "he wants them to leave".

This rule is bad because it does not indicate which verb (want or go) should be tagged as subjunctive, it does not explain how the other verb should be tagged, and it does not refer to the syntax of the clause, only the meaning.

Here is an improved version of this rule which describes the syntax in the object language.

3: Tag a subclause a verb as subjunctive if it reflects a desire or belief in a subclause introduced with "ut" or a relative pronoun. Tag verbs in subclauses with no introductory particle as infinitives.

vult eos abesse
want-3SG 3PL be.absent-INF

vult ut abessent
want-3SG COMP be.absent-3PL.SBJV

State three to five rules, using this format.

One output from this prompt, as produced by ChatGPT, is given below.

Certainly! Here are some rules for distinguishing between the PFV.CVB and PST.UNW tags in Tsez:

1. **Tag a verb as PFV.CVB if it appears in a subordinate clause that provides background information or context for the main action, often preceding the main verb.** The PFV.CVB verb typically describes an action that is completed before the action of the main verb. For example:

- Sentence: *Babiya uži Okude sadaq egirno xecin.*
- Gloss: dad-ERG son Oku-APUD.ESS together send-PFV.CVB leave-PST.UNW
- Translation: "The father sent his son together with Oku."

In this sentence, "egirno" (send-PFV.CVB) provides context for the main action "xecin" (leave-PST.UNW).

2. **Tag a verb as PST.UNW if it is the main verb of the sentence, indicating the primary action or event that is being reported.** The PST.UNW verb typically follows the PFV.CVB verb if both are present in the sentence. For example:

- Sentence: *Žedu teɫ iduɣor boqnosi, ceyä beħiqus uži žeduz ɣ^{ʕ}utkoxor egirno.*
- Gloss: DEM1.IPL inside home-IN.ALL III-become-ANT.CVB eagle-ERG hunter-GEN1 son DEM1.IPL.OBL-GEN2 house-AD.LAT let-PST.UNW
- Translation: "When they had gone into their house, the eagle let the hunter's son down to their house."

In this sentence, "egirno" (let-PST.UNW) is the main action reported.

3. **Tag a verb as PFV.CVB if it appears in a sequence of actions where it indicates a completed

action that leads to or results in the subsequent action.** The PFV.CVB verb often precedes another verb that is tagged as PST.UNW. For example:

- Sentence: *Kʷaxatow sida igozo ʕaƛay nesi žax ɬet'in sis bercinaw kidno yown.*
- Gloss: soon-EMPH one.OBL near-ATTR.OBL village-IN.ABL DEM1.ISG.OBL boy-AD.ESS pick-PFV.CVB one beautiful girl-TOP II-marry-PST.UNW
- Translation: "Soon, that boy picked a beautiful girl from the neighboring village and married her."

In this sentence, "ɬet'in" (pick-PFV.CVB) is a completed action that leads to "yown" (marry-PST.UNW).

4. **Tag a verb as PST.UNW if it is used to report a past event or action that has relevance to the narrative or discourse context.** The PST.UNW verb often concludes a sequence of actions or provides the main point of the sentence. For example:

- Sentence: *Xaner iyn anu yeda nesis uži yaɬruɬi.*
- Gloss: khan-LAT know-PST.UNW be.NEG DEM2.ISG DEM1.ISG.OBL-GEN1 son be-MSD
- Translation: "The king didn't know that he was his own son."

In this sentence, "iyn" (know-PST.UNW) reports the main event of the narrative.

5. **Tag a verb as PFV.CVB if it is used in a conditional or hypothetical clause, providing a condition or premise for the main action.** The PFV.CVB verb often appears before a PST.UNW verb that describes the outcome or result. For example:

- Sentence: *Nedur resunäyƛin, eƛin užä dahawcen ičin, mažgityaɣorno ik'ač'in, idun kecač'in.*
- Gloss: so IV-exist-CND.CVB-QUOT say-PST.UNW boy-ERG a.little-EQU1-TOP wait-PFV.CVB mosque-IN.VERS-and go-NEG.FUT.DEF home-and sleep-NEG.FUT.DEF
- Translation: "'If that's the case,' said the boy, 'I'll wait a little, and will neither go to the mosque, nor sleep here at home."

In this sentence, "eƛin" (say-PST.UNW) is the main action, while "dahawcen" (wait-PFV.CVB) provides a condition for the subsequent actions.

These criteria may be compared with the grammar as follows:

1. Subordinate clause verbs are converbs: Correct. "The majority of Tsez adverbial clauses have a converb as their predicate" (Polinsky, 2014, p.296).

2. Main verb is PST.UNW: Correct.

3. Converbs in sequence of actions indicating actions that lead to the main action: Correct. Polinsky describes these as "clause chains" (p.297).

4. PST.UNW used to report a past event relevant to the discourse: True but vague. Polinsky agrees that PST.UNW generally has past reference (p.298) but also states that it should be used for a 2nd/3rd person subject due to its evidential status. Tense cannot be used to identify the PST.UNW because the converb also often has past tense reference, although it is not required to do so.

5. Converbs in hypothetical: Mostly incorrect. Tsez uses specialized converbs for hypothetical constructions (p.314-315) rather than using the PFV.CVB. However, PFV.CVB can appear in hypotheticals due to "linking of converbs, where only one converb is marked as conditional but takes adjoined converbs under its scope, [the] preferred option of expressing that several events are viewed as hypothetical or counterfactual." (p.315) GPT's example does not seem to clearly fit this criterion, since although it states that "wait a little" is part of the hypothetical clause, it is actually part of the consequent ("If that's the case, [then] I'll wait. . . ").

F Chain of thought outputs

We show here some additional examples of how GPT-4 applies the guidelines for distinguishing finite verbs and converbs. In the following case, our basic system mislabels 'come' as a converb but the instruction-augmented system correctly labels it as a finite verb.

(5) Ayn yeda sidaɣ
come-*PST.UNW* DEM2.ISG in.one.place
bʕeliz ciqɬer.
poplar-GEN2 forest-CONT.LAT
'He came to a poplar forest.'

An excerpt from the chain of thought shows that the 'main verb' criterion is correctly applied:

2. **PST.UNW as the main verb**: "Ayn" is likely the main verb of the sentence, as it describes the primary action of coming to a poplar forest. There is no other verb in the sentence that would serve as the main verb, which supports the use of PST.UNW.

In the following case, our basic system mislabels 'hear' as a finite verb, but the instruction-augmented system correctly labels it as a converb.

(6) Žedus xabarno
DEM1.IPL.OBL-GEN1 story-TOP
teqno žeduɬ
hear-PFV.CVB DEM1.IPL.OBL-CONT.ESS

xizay iłetow c'odorawni esiwn
behind as-EMPH clever-DEF brother-*TOP*
ik'in.
go-PST.UNW

'Having heard their talking, the clever brother went behind them likewise.'

Below, an excerpt from the chain of thought correctly indicates that 'hear' is not the main verb and appears earlier in the string, both indicating the CVB tag.

Now, let's apply the guidelines:

1. **PFV.CVB in subordinate clauses**: The word "teqno" appears before the main verb "ik'in" (go-PST.UNW). This suggests that "teqno" could be providing background information or context for the main action, which aligns with the use of PFV.CVB.

2. **PST.UNW as the main verb**: The main action of the sentence is "ik'in" (go-PST.UNW), which indicates the primary event. "Teqno" is not the main verb here, which makes it less likely to be PST.UNW.

3. **PFV.CVB in sequences of actions**: The sentence describes a sequence where the clever brother hears something and then goes behind them. "Teqno" could represent a completed action that leads to the subsequent action "ik'in" (go-PST.UNW), supporting the use of PFV.CVB.

In the following case, the instruction-augmented system makes a mistake due to misrecognition of the main verb and labels 'do' as a converb rather than a main verb.

(7) Boƛƛo zaman bik'inosi
III-middle time III-go-ANT.CVB
bara xediw bet'erbaqi boda
wife-ERG husband life III-do-INF
ik'anix muk'ur oyn
go-MSD-AD.ESS confess *do-PST.UNW*

'After some time has passed, the wife confessed that she went to live with her husband.'

The chain of thought produced by ChatGPT labels 'persuade', which is not inflected, as the main verb, and *oyn* as a subordinate verb— in fact, it acts as the head (auxiliary) verb. The issue, as discussed in the main text, is that ChatGPT tends to prioritize the English translation over the Tsez sentence— the instructions state that "the PST.UNW verb typically follows the PFV.CVB verb if both are present", but also that the "main verb" should be tagged as PST.UNW. Here, the information about ordering (which would have given the right answer) is deemphasized in favor of the "main verb" criterion, which is incorrect due to the auxiliary. (The inferred tag sequence is shown in the excerpt. The retrieval system retrieves the primary meaning 'persuade' rather than 'confess' for *muk'ur*, but this is corrected in the final gloss.)

Translation: 1. **Boƛƛo** - noun (III-middle)
2. **zaman** - noun (time)
3. **bik'inosi** - verb (I.PL-go-ANT.CVB)
4. **bara** - noun (wife-ERG)
5. **xediw** - noun (husband)
6. **bet'erbaqi** - noun (life)
7. **boda** - verb (III-do-INF)
8. **ik'anix** - verb (go-MSD-AD.ESS)
9. **muk'ur** - verb (persuade)
10. **oyn** - verb (?)

1. **PFV.CVB in subordinate clauses**: The candidate gloss suggests that "bik'inosi" (I.PL-go-ANT.CVB) is a subordinate clause providing background information. The main action seems to be the wife's confession about going to live with her husband. "Oyn" could potentially be a PFV.CVB if it provides context or background to the main action.

...

West Germanic noun-noun compounds and the morphology-syntax trade-off

Pablo Mosteiro
Utrecht University
Utrecht, the Netherlands
p.mosteiro@uu.nl

Damián Blasi
Pompeu Fabra University
Barcelona, Spain
dblasi@fas.harvard.edu

Denis Paperno
Utrecht University
Utrecht, the Netherlands
d.paperno@uu.nl

Abstract

This paper examines the linguistic distinction between syntax and morphology, focusing on noun-noun compounds in three West Germanic languages (English, Dutch, and German). Previous studies using the Parallel Bible Corpus have found a trade-off between word order (syntax) and word structure (morphology), with languages optimizing information conveyance through these systems. Our research question is whether manipulating English noun-noun compounds to resemble Dutch and German constructions can reproduce the observed distance between these languages in the order-structure plane. We extend a word-pasting procedure to merge increasingly common noun-noun pairs in English Bible translations. After each merge, we estimate the information contained in word order and word structure using entropy calculations. Our results show that pasting noun-noun pairs reduces the difference between English and the other languages, suggesting that orthographic conventions defining word boundaries play a role in this distinction. However, the effect is not pronounced, and results are statistically inconclusive.

1 Introduction

The linguistic distinction between *syntax* and *morphology* is well-known and contentious (Tallman and Auderset, 2023; Crystal, 2010). Syntax is often understood as the study of word combinations into phrases and sentences, while morphology focuses on internal word processes. However, the boundary between these domains is blurred, and attempts to distinguish them often hinge on the complex notion of *wordhood* (Haspelmath, 2023). Some patterns in language, nonetheless, seem to support a morphology-syntax divide, with languages relying more on one or the other system.

Previous research using the Parallel Bible Corpus (PBC) (Mayer and Cysouw, 2014) found this trade-off across many languages, suggesting that languages optimize information conveyance through these systems (Koplenig et al., 2017). More recently, Mosteiro and Blasi (2025) postulated that the statistical order-structure trade-off observed could be ascribed to the conventional word boundaries used in the curation of the dataset.

We focus on a phenomenon straddling the border between morphology and syntax: noun-noun compounds in West Germanic languages. While Dutch and German form noun-noun compounds by creating a single orthographic word, English conventionally writes noun-noun compounds as separate words. For example, the expression *winter garden* is two words in English, but its equivalents *wintertuin* and *Wintergarten* in Dutch and German, respectively, are composed of one word. At the surface level, the English construction seems syntactic, while the Dutch and German constructions seems morphological. Noun-noun compounds have been the subject of extensive linguistic study (Sun and Harald Baayen, 2021; Gast, 2008; Berg, 2006).

Our research question is: **can we reproduce the distance between English on the one hand and Dutch and German on the other in the study by Koplenig et al. (2017) by manipulating English noun-noun compounds, so that they stick together as in Dutch and German?**

To answer this question, we reproduce the word-pasting experiment of Mosteiro and Blasi (2025), but this time we only allow word pairs to be merged if both of the words involved are nouns. Thus, we investigate whether the observed distance between English and Dutch/German in the order-structure plane is merely an artifact of orthographic conventions defining word boundaries.

2 Materials and Methods

We use a multilingual parallel corpus, on which we apply a word-pasting methodology (Mosteiro and Blasi, 2025) to paste common word-pairs to-

Proceedings of the The 22nd SIGMORPHON workshop on Computational Morphology, Phonology, and Phonetics, pages 15–22
May 3, 2025 ©2025 Association for Computational Linguistics

gether, and then we compute the amount of information contained in word-order and word-structure using an entropy estimator based on Shannon's entropy (Shannon, 1948; Koplenig et al., 2017). [1]

2.1 Data

We use the Parallel Bible Corpus (Mayer and Cysouw, 2014), which comprises 2000 translations of the Bible in 1460 languages, covering over 40 language families worldwide[2]. Each translation is preprocessed with tokenization, Unicode normalization, and insertion of spaces between words and punctuation. As in Koplenig et al. (2017), we split translations into individual books, and focus on six New Testament books (Matthew, Mark, Luke, John, Acts, and Revelation). We do not lowercase the texts in the preprocessing step, and instead do this after part-of-speech tagging. We only consider bibles in Dutch, German, or English, as indicated by file names starting in `nld`, `deu`, or `eng`, respectively. Because contemporary German only became fully standardized in the 19th century, we exclude bibles translated before 1800. We only included bibles that contained at least 90% of all the indexed verses in each of the six books considered. Our final dataset consists of 23 bible translations in German, 29 in English, and 4 in Dutch. The list of bible translations can be found in Appendix A.

2.2 Part-of-speech tagging

We employ part-of-speech (POS) tagging to identify nouns in our datasets, utilizing SpaCy's `en_core_web_lg` model, version 3.8.0, for its large size and CPU-optimization. POS tagging is applied to English data only, while German and Dutch data are excluded due to the subsequent omission of the word-pasting algorithm on those languages. For each token, we extract the Universal POS (UPOS) tag to classify words as nouns (`NOUN`) or otherwise. After POS tagging, we lowercase all tokens as in Koplenig et al. (2017).

2.3 Entropy calculator

Following the work of Koplenig et al. (2017), we aim to estimate the amount of information carried by word order and word structure, which are proxies for syntax and morphology. To do this, we create three versions of each bible translation. One is the original text, named `orig`. The second version, named *shuffled*, is obtained by shuffling all tokens within each verse in the text. This effectively destroys word order. The third version, named *masked*, is obtained by replacing each word type in a book by a unique randomly generated character sequence of the same length. This effectively destroys word structure. An example is shown on Table 1. After applying these operations at the verse level, all verses in a book are concatenated in a shuffled manner, thus creating an original, a shuffled, and a masked version of each book. Each of these versions is fed into an entropy calculator (Koplenig et al., 2017), which returns the amount of information contained in each of these versions, in bits per unit character. This results in the quantities H^b_{original}, H^b_{order}, and $H^b_{\text{structure}}$, corresponding to the `orig`, `shuffled`, and `masked` versions of book b, respectively. We then compute the information contained in word order and word structure as:

$$D^b_{\text{order}} = H^b_{\text{order}} - H^b_{\text{orig}} \quad (1)$$

$$D^b_{\text{structure}} = H^b_{\text{structure}} - H^b_{\text{orig}} \quad (2)$$

2.4 Word pasting

We replicate and extend the word-pasting experiment from Mosteiro and Blasi (2025) on English Bible translations. For each book in each translation, we iteratively generate new versions by merging the most frequent noun-noun word pair into a compound. Following each merge, we create original, shuffled, and masked versions of each book and compute estimates of D^b_{order} and $D^b_{\text{structure}}$ using the entropy calculator introduced in Section 2.3. We do not paste proper nouns, as exploratory analysis showed limited pasting of proper nouns in German and Dutch[3]. This splitting methodology is applied solely to English translations.

2.5 Final pipeline

We take the 56 bible translations described in Section 2.1. Following previous work (Koplenig et al., 2017), we consider only six books of the New Testament. We thus arrive at 342 book-translation pairs. We split each of these into verses and create an original, a masked, and a shuffled version of it. We then paste the verses back together to obtain an original, a masked, and a shuffled version of each book-translation. We feed each of these into an entropy calculator to obtain the information in bits

[1] All our code can be found at `https://github.com/PabloMosUU/WordOrderBibles`.

[2] We use commit `9e66cf47f`. Newer versions contain even more translations.

[3] For example, English *Jesus Christ* is *Jezus Christus* in Dutch and *Jesus Christus* in German.

Version	Text
orig	`immediately` **`they`** `left the boat and` **`their`** `father and followed him .`
shuffled	`followed boat him and the and father` **`their they`** `left . immediately`
masked	`aihuraovaha` **`phun`** `fafa luh avnn wso` **`octaa`** `otstsh wso tehreaed fed e`

Table 1: Three versions of each verse of the bible are created before computing the entropy in bits per unit character of each book. The **boldface** merely highlights the effect, by showing that two words that are related in both their form and their meaning in the original text are mapped to completely different words in the masked text.

per character, then we compute two differences to obtain the information contained in word order and word structure for each book-translation. In the case of English, we expand this analysis by pasting noun-noun pairs iteratively from the most common to the least common and recomputing the word-order and word-structure information at each step. For each language, book, and number of merges[4], we average the values of D^b_{order} and $D^b_{\text{structure}}$, as in Koplenig et al. (2017).

Book	Max verses	Max NN merges
Acts	1007	34.5
John	879	23.7
Luke	1151	48.9
Mark	678	28.8
Matthew	1071	43.5
Revelation	404	28.4

Table 2: For each book considered, the maximum number of verses found across the available English translations, and the maximum number of noun-noun merges, averaged over translations.

3 Results

Figure 1 shows our main result. The red squares and green stars are the word-order and word-structure information for Dutch (`nld`) and German (`deu`), respectively. The blue dot labeled "eng-orig" corresponds to the average of the original English bible translations. The blue dot labeled "eng-nn-pasted" is the average value of word-order and word-structure information across English translations after all noun-noun pairs have been pasted together. For comparison, the cyan triangles are reproductions of Mosteiro and Blasi (2025), in which the first 100 and 200 most common word pairs have been pasted together, regardless of POS tag. The fit line shown is the one found by Koplenig et al. (2017) by fitting an inverse proportionality line on word-order and word-structure information across all languages in the PBC. The number of noun-noun merges required for each book to reach the point when no more noun-noun pairs can be pasted, averaged over translations, is shown on Table 2. In Appendix B we report the results of repeating the study using SpaCy's `en_core_web_trf`, a transformer model. Qualitatively we observed similar results.

[4]For German and Dutch, we do not do any merging, so we average values of D^b_{order} and $D^b_{\text{structure}}$ for each language and book.

4 Discussion

Figure 1 indicates that pasting noun-noun pairs together either leaves the English data point unchanged brings it closer to the Dutch and German data points. The effect is much smaller than when we paste all words regardless of POS tag. For Acts and John, no effect is observable altogether. Table 2 shows the maximum number of verses for each book in English. Note that Acts and John are neither the longest nor the shortest books, so there a priori no reason to believe that the effect should be smaller or negligible for those books.

Let $\Delta(D_{\text{order}})$ and $\Delta(D_{\text{structure}})$ be the differences between D_{order} and $D_{\text{structure}}$, respectively, before and after the noun-pasting procedure. Table 3 shows the values of $\Delta(D_{\text{order}})$ and $\Delta(D_{\text{structure}})$ across the various translations in English, together with the p-value for a paired permutation test to discard a null hypothesis in which both Δ is 0. From this table, we can conclude that only $\Delta(D_{\text{structure}})$ in Revelation is significantly different from 0.

It would be desirable to study longer corpora, not only because it would allow more noun-noun pairs to be pasted, but also because the entropy estimator we used converges to the entropy for long texts (Kontoyiannis et al., 1998). Convergence was checked in a previous study (Koplenig et al., 2017). Still, in future work we plan to evaluate

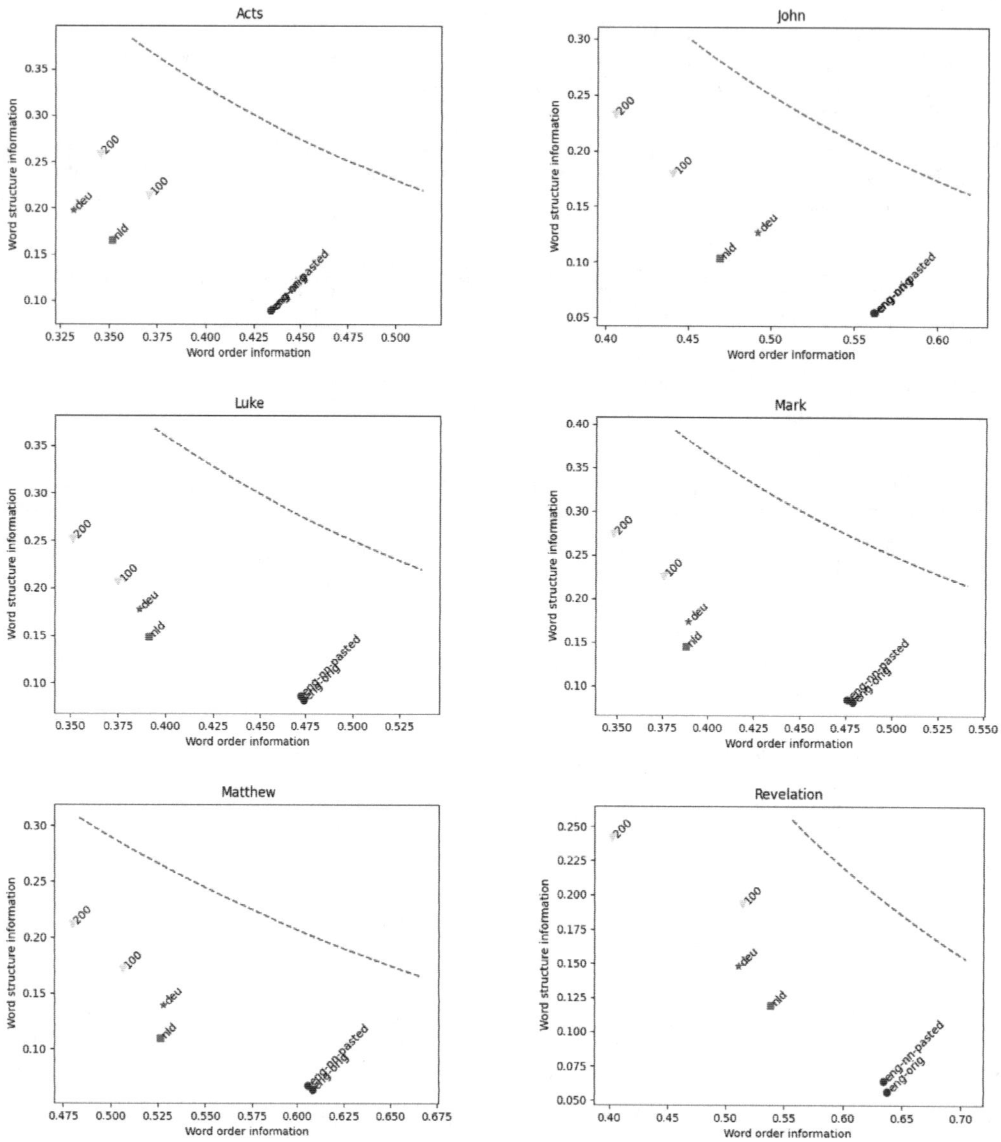

Figure 1: Word-structure versus word-order information for English, Dutch, and German. The green stars and red squares are German (deu) and Dutch (`nld`), respectively. The blue dots are English data, before (`eng-orig`) and after (`eng-nn-pasted`) pasting all noun-noun pairs in the book together. The cyan triangles are obtained by pasting the 100 and 200 most common word pairs regardless of POS tag. The dashed line is the best fit found by Koplenig et al. (2017) using all languages in the Parallel Bible Corpus.

these quantities over multiple books combined.

Although the evidence is not conclusive, there seems to be an indication that pasting noun-noun pairs together, which implicitly turns English noun-noun compounds from two words into one, brings the English word-order and word-structure information closer to the values for Dutch and German.

Future work will use word splitting (Mosteiro and Blasi, 2025) to split Dutch and German noun-noun compounds and evaluate whether the data points move closer to the English data points.

5 Conclusions

In conclusion, our study aimed to investigate whether the observed distance between English and Dutch/German in the order-structure plane, as reported by Koplenig et al. (2017), is merely an

Book	Metric	Δ	p
Acts	D_{order}	-0.00074	0.470
	$D_{\text{structure}}$	-0.00164	0.648
John	D_{order}	-0.00071	0.473
	$D_{\text{structure}}$	0.00002	0.497
Luke	D_{order}	-0.00155	0.438
	$D_{\text{structure}}$	0.00445	0.146
Mark	D_{order}	-0.00291	0.391
	$D_{\text{structure}}$	0.00334	0.234
Matthew	D_{order}	-0.00233	0.426
	$D_{\text{structure}}$	0.00358	0.139
Revelation	D_{order}	-0.00310	0.356
	$D_{\text{structure}}$	0.00816	0.006

Table 3: $\Delta(D_{\text{order}})$ and $\Delta(D_{\text{structure}})$ for each book as estimated by a paired permutation test in which each paired sample consists of D_{order} and $D_{\text{structure}}$ for a single English translation, before and after merging noun-noun pairs, for a total of 29 paired datapoints. We used 100000 resamples. Only the p-value for $D_{\text{structure}}$ for Revelation is less than 0.05, meaning that noun-noun merges caused a statistically significant increase in $D_{\text{structure}}$ for Revelation.

artifact of orthographic conventions defining word boundaries. By replicating and extending the word-pasting experiment from Mosteiro and Blasi (2025) on English Bible translations, we found that pasting increasingly common noun-noun pairs together reduces the difference between English and the other languages, suggesting that the distinction is at least partially due to this factor.

However, the effect was not as pronounced as observed in the original study due to a small number of noun-noun pairs present in the corpus (see Table 2), and the shift was not statistically significant. This small effect could also be caused by the fact that the words we pasted are less frequent than those pasted by Mosteiro and Blasi (2025), because we selected a subset of their words. Future work will check this effect on a bigger corpus with more noun-noun pairs.

Limitations

In this study we applied POS tagging at the individual verse level. Future work could check whether tagging entire books of the bible would increase POS-tagging performance.

We used commit `9e66cf47f` of the PBC for consistency with prior work. There might be additional bible translations in our languages of interest in more recent versions of the PBC.

Not all noun-noun clusters in English are compounded in their German or Dutch translations. But in our study we pasted all occurring pairs of nouns. A refinement of this work would check that all noun-noun pairs pasted are linguistically accurate, in the sense that their counterparts in German or Dutch would be compounds.

As for the linguistic question, we only considered one phenomenon in one language family, namely noun-noun compounds in West Germanic languages. It would be interesting to find another phenomenon occurring in another language family, to validate our methodology.

References

Thomas Berg. 2006. The internal structure of four-noun compounds in english and german. *Corpus Linguistics and Linguistic Theory*, 2(2):197–231.

David Crystal. 2010. *The Cambridge encyclopedia of language*. Cambridge University Press Cambridge.

Volker Gast. 2008. Verb-noun compounds in english and german. *Zeitschrift für Anglistik und Amerikanistik*, 56(3):269–282.

Martin Haspelmath. 2023. Defining the word. *Word*, 69(3):283–297.

Ioannis Kontoyiannis, Paul Algoet, Yuri Suhov, and Abraham Wyner. 1998. Nonparametric Entropy Estimation for Stationary Processesand Random Fields, with Applications to English Text. *Information Theory, IEEE Transactions on*, 44:1319 – 1327.

Alexander Koplenig, Peter Meyer, Sascha Wolfer, and Carolin Müller-Spitzer. 2017. The statistical trade-off between word order and word structure – Large-scale evidence for the principle of least effort. *PLOS ONE*, 12(3):1–25. Publisher: Public Library of Science.

Thomas Mayer and Michael Cysouw. 2014. Creating a massively parallel bible corpus. In *Proceedings of the Ninth International Conference on Language Resources and Evaluation (LREC'14)*, Reykjavik, Iceland. European Language Resources Association (ELRA).

Pablo Mosteiro and Damián Blasi. 2025. Word boundaries and the morphology-syntax trade-off. In *Proceedings of the New Horizons in Computational Linguistics for Religious Texts*, pages 86–93, Abu Dhabi, UAE. Association for Computational Linguistics.

C. E. Shannon. 1948. A mathematical theory of communication. *Bell System Technical Journal*, 27(3):379–423.

Kun Sun and R. Harald Baayen. 2021. Hyphenation as a compounding technique in english. *Language Sciences*, 83:101326.

Book	Max verses	Max NN merges
Acts	1007	40.1
John	879	28.0
Luke	1151	54.8
Mark	678	35.0
Matthew	1071	50.3
Revelation	404	28.4

Table 4: Maximum number of noun-noun merges for each book, averaged across English translations. Compared to Table 2, this one was generated using SpaCy's transformer model `en_core_web_trf` as a POS tagger instead of `en_core_web_lg`. The **Max verses** column is unchanged because that is a property of the input texts.

Adam JR Tallman and Sandra Auderset. 2023. Measuring and assessing indeterminacy and variation in the morphology-syntax distinction. *Linguistic Typology*, 27(1):113–156.

A List of bibles used

Table 5 shows the file names of the bible translations used for this study.

B Transformer-based POS tagger

We repeated the entire analysis of this paper using SpaCy's `en_core_web_trf`, a transformer model, instead of `en_core_web_lg`. The results are shown on Figure 2 and Table 4. We note that the average number of noun-noun pairs is higher than with `en_core_web_lg`. This means that either the `en_core_web_lg` model incorrectly classifies nouns as other parts of speech, or that `en_core_web_trf` incorrectly selects non-nouns as nouns. However, the figure shows that the downstream results are slightly less significant than those found with `en_core_web_lg` (Figure 1).

Translation name	
deu-x-bible-albrecht.txt	deu-x-bible-elberfelder1871.txt
deu-x-bible-elberfelder1905.txt	deu-x-bible-freebible.txt
deu-x-bible-genfer2011.txt	deu-x-bible-greber.txt
deu-x-bible-gruenewalder.txt	deu-x-bible-interlinear.txt
deu-x-bible-konkordant.txt	deu-x-bible-lebendig.txt
deu-x-bible-luther1912.txt	deu-x-bible-luther2017.txt
deu-x-bible-meister.txt	deu-x-bible-menge.txt
deu-x-bible-neue.txt	deu-x-bible-newworld.txt
deu-x-bible-pattloch.txt	deu-x-bible-schlachter.txt
deu-x-bible-schlachter2000.txt	deu-x-bible-tafelbibel.txt
deu-x-bible-textbibel.txt	deu-x-bible-volxbibel.txt
deu-x-bible-zuercher.txt	eng-x-bible-amplified.txt
eng-x-bible-basic.txt	eng-x-bible-catholic.txt
eng-x-bible-clontz.txt	eng-x-bible-common.txt
eng-x-bible-darby.txt	eng-x-bible-diaglot.txt
eng-x-bible-easytoread.txt	eng-x-bible-etheridge.txt
eng-x-bible-godsword.txt	eng-x-bible-goodnews.txt
eng-x-bible-lexham.txt	eng-x-bible-literal.txt
eng-x-bible-majority.txt	eng-x-bible-modern.txt
eng-x-bible-montgomery.txt	eng-x-bible-new2007.txt
eng-x-bible-newcentury.txt	eng-x-bible-newinternational.txt
eng-x-bible-newliving.txt	eng-x-bible-newreaders.txt
eng-x-bible-newsimplified.txt	eng-x-bible-newworld1984.txt
eng-x-bible-newworld2013.txt	eng-x-bible-passion.txt
eng-x-bible-riverside.txt	eng-x-bible-treeoflife.txt
eng-x-bible-world.txt	eng-x-bible-worldwide.txt
nld-x-bible-1951.txt	nld-x-bible-2004.txt
nld-x-bible-2007.txt	nld-x-bible-newworld.txt

Table 5: Bible translations from the PBC that were used in the present study.

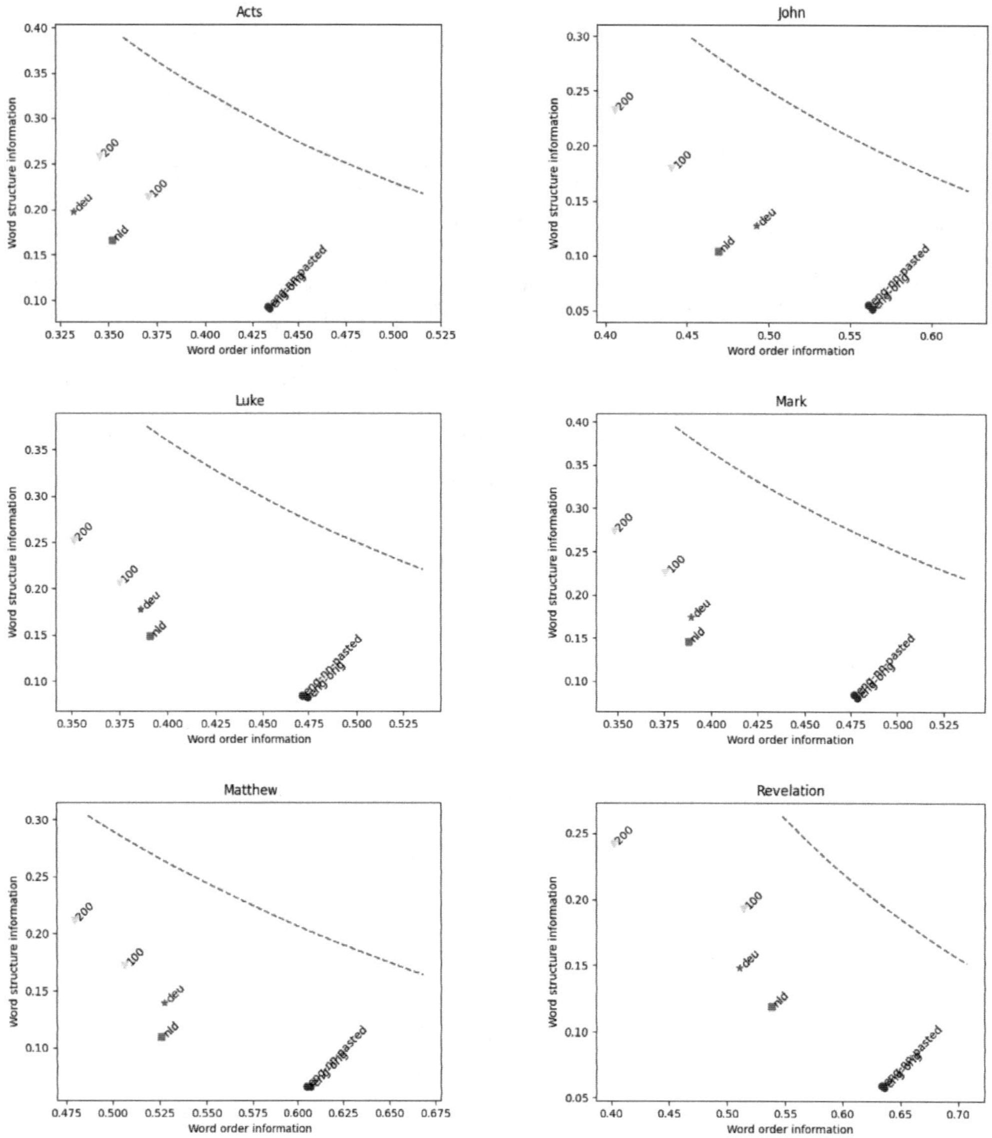

Figure 2: The same analysis as presented in Figure 1, this time using SpaCy's transformer model en_core_web_trf instead of en_core_web_lg.

The Impact of Dialect Variation on Robust Automatic Speech Recognition for Catalan

Zachary Hopton and **Eleanor Chodroff**
{zacharywilliam.hopton,eleanor.chodroff}@uzh.ch
University of Zurich

Abstract

To accurately transcribe a speech signal, automatic speech recognition (ASR) systems must show robustness to a wide range of task-independent variation, such as speaker factors, recording quality, or even "adversarial noise" designed to disrupt performance.We manipulated the dialect composition of fine-tuning data for ASR to study whether balancing the relative proportion of dialects had an impact on models' robustness to two such sources of variation: dialect variation and adversarial perturbations. We fine-tuned XLSR-53 for Catalan ASR using four different dialect compositions, each containing the Central Catalan dialect. These were defined as 100%, 80%, 50%, and 20% Central Catalan, with the remaining portions split evenly between four other Catalan dialects. While increasing the relative proportion of dialect variants improved models' dialect robustness, this did not have a meaningful impact on adversarial robustness. These findings suggest that while improvements to ASR can be made by diversifying the training data, such changes do not sufficiently counteract adversarial attacks, leaving the technology open to security threats.

https://github.com/zhopto3/DialAttack

1 Introduction

Effectively handling dialect variation is an important attribute of a high-performing automatic speech recognition system. While incorporating dialect variation into a model's training data may benefit this robustness (Jie et al., 2024; Dan et al., 2022; Lonergan et al., 2023), the relative lack of speech data with clean accent or dialect labels poses a challenge for this line of research. Moreover, the exact approach to incorporating data from other dialects could have consequences beyond just the model's ASR performance. Research on the robustness of neural networks to adversarial attacks has indicated that unbalanced training datasets may result in models that are more susceptible to adversarial attacks (Wu et al., 2021; Richards et al., 2023). When evaluating the susceptibility of Open AI's Whisper to adversarial noise, Olivier and Raj (2023) found that attacks on the model's language identification token were more effective when the attack's language was less present in the model's training data. For models trained on data from mutually intelligible dialects, it is an open question as to whether an unbalanced dataset would increase susceptibility to adversarial attacks. Training on multiple dialects may even confer a robustness to adversarial noise, analogous to training models on geometrically transformed or adversarial examples (Silva and Najafirad, 2020).

Catalan's well-documented dialect variation makes it a good candidate for studying questions of multi-dialect ASR (Veny, 2015, 1982; Calvo and Segura-Llopes, 2022). A great deal of research has focused on the compilation of Catalan corpora (Kjartansson et al., 2020; Kulebi et al., 2022; Boleda et al., 2006; Ljubešić and Toral, 2014). Catalan also has a substantial presence in the Common Voice corpus, for which diverse speakers of the language write, record, and validate data points on a voluntary basis (Ardila et al., 2020). Catalan's presence in Common Voice has grown substantially in recent releases of the corpus thanks to data management and campaigning efforts from a number of bodies (Armentano-Oller et al., 2024). Notable among these efforts is the encouragement of Catalan speakers with various accents to contribute to the corpus, and to include their accent in the metadata of the recording.

Here we use data from five Catalan dialects to answer two questions about multi-dialect ASR: First, to what extent is balancing the quantity of data from different dialects necessary when training models meant to accurately transcribe multiple varieties of a language? And second, does training an ASR

Proceedings of the The 22nd SIGMORPHON workshop on Computational Morphology, Phonology, and Phonetics, pages 23–33
May 3, 2025 ©2025 Association for Computational Linguistics

model on an unbalanced dataset with multiple dialects impact the model's security at inference?

2 Methods

2.1 Multi-dialect Catalan Speech Recognition

The first step of our experiments consisted of fine-tuning XLSR-53 for Catalan ASR (Conneau et al., 2021). We used XLSR-53 instead of a later version of XLSR since Catalan was not part of the pretraining data for this model, eliminating a potential confound in the manipulation of the dialect composition in the fine-tuning data[1].

Our data source was the validated portion of Catalan Common Voice 18.0[2] (Ardila et al., 2020). Similar to Armentano-Oller et al. (2024), we first mapped each unique accent label for a given audio file to one of five Catalan macro-dialects: Balearic, Central, Nord, Nord-Occidental, and Valencià. Audio files from second language learners were excluded, as were underspecified accent responses such as "Catalan" or "normative."

We then sampled four training and development datasets with 100%, 80%, 50%, and 20% Central Catalan; the remaining portion of each set was split evenly between the other four dialects. This meant that the 20% Central train and development datasets were perfectly balanced with respect to the five macro-dialects studied. We randomly sampled a single test set from the remaining data with an equal number of samples from each macro-dialect. Figure 2 shows the final proportion of each dialect in the four models' training data. All four models were fine-tuned on 152 hours of data with 19 hours of development data. This training set size is comparable to previous work that has used XLSR for multi-dialect speech processing (Zuluaga-Gomez et al., 2023; Lonergan et al., 2023). See Appendix A for fine-tuning details.

2.2 Robustness to Adversarial Noise

After training our ASR models, we randomly selected 50 audio files from each dialect's evaluation set to train a total of 250 adversarial attacks on each of the four models. Put generally, we aimed to add noise to our input audio files that resulted in the model outputting an adversarial target—"Porta'm a un lloc web malvat," or "Take me to an evil website"—despite the perceivable audio input saying something else. More specifically, we trained targeted, adversarial noise δ for a given audio file x as in Carlini and Wagner (2018). In such Carlini-and-Wagner (CW) attacks, the objective is also to make the noise relatively imperceptible. As in Olivier and Raj (2023), we judged the perceptibility of the noise relative to the signal in decibels using the signal-to-noise ratio (SNR), but using the L_∞ metric, similar to Carlini and Wagner (2018):

$$\mathrm{SNR}(x, \delta) = 20(\log |x|_\infty - \log |\delta|_\infty) \quad (1)$$

For details on the algorithm and hyperparameters used to train the adversarial noise δ, see Appendix B.

2.3 Evaluation

Following fine-tuning, we ran inference over the withheld test set of Catalan data. Each ASR model was evaluated on the same 19-hour evaluation dataset with equal representation from each dialect (2486 audio files per dialect).

To assess variation in WER and CER, a generalized linear model for a gamma-distributed dependent variable was implemented in R, using the identity link function. The model included main effects of the model dialect composition (100%, 80%, 50%, or 20% Central Catalan), the speech input dialect (Balear, Central, Nord, Nord-Occidental, or Valencià), and the interaction between the model dialect composition and speech dialect. A gamma distribution was chosen given that the WER and CER distributions have a strong positive skew and cannot be negative.[3] Each predictor was sum-coded with the held-out levels first set to the 100% Central model and the Catalan test files, and then rotated to test each main effect and interaction against the average performance.

To evaluate the effectiveness of the CW attacks on each fine-tuned model, we primarily use the percentage of successful attacks. An attack was considered successful if—at any SNR—the WER of the model output compared to the adversarial target ("Porta'm a un lloc web malvat.") was 0. To assess the influences on a successful or unsuccessful attack, we implemented a binomial logistic regression model with fixed effects of dialect, the fine-tuning data composition of the model, and

[1] https://github.com/facebookresearch/fairseq/tree/main/examples/wav2vec

[2] https://commonvoice.mozilla.org/en/datasets

[3] As the gamma prediction can only predict positive values greater than 0, we transformed any WER or CER of 0 in our data to 0.00001.

	WER					CER				
	bal	cen	nor	no-oc	val	bal	cen	nor	no-oc	val
100%	0.280	0.152	0.191	0.244	0.234	0.079	0.038	0.049	0.064	0.056
80%	0.224	0.146	0.160	0.196	0.165	0.060	0.037	0.040	0.050	0.039
50%	**0.181**	**0.140**	**0.133**	0.164	0.126	**0.047**	**0.035**	**0.033**	**0.041**	**0.029**
20%	0.189	0.164	0.144	**0.161**	**0.125**	0.050	0.043	0.036	0.042	0.035

Table 1: Percentages in the far left column represent the percent Central Catalan data used in fine-tuning; bal: Balearic, cen: Central, nor: Nord, no-oc: Nord-Occidental, val: Valencià; Bold: lowest WER/CER for each dialect.

their interaction. Categorical predictors were sum-coded.

3 Results

3.1 ASR

In terms of WER and CER, ASR for all dialects improved with more dialect-balanced data (Table 1). The WER model revealed significant influences of model composition and dialect input: relative to average, the 20% and 50% Central models had significantly lower WERs, while the 100% Central model had significantly higher WERs across all dialects. The average performance across models was significantly better on Central, Nord and València, but worse on Balear and Nord-Occidental. The main effects were significantly tempered in several interactions; a significant interaction can be interpreted as a significant modulation from the expected WER performance based on the main effects alone. Beyond the main effects, the 20% Central model performed significantly better on Balear, Nord-Occidental, and València, but worse on Central and Nord. The 50% Central model also performed significantly better on Balear and València, but the main effect of the 50% Central model was significantly tempered for the Central test files: While the Central WER of the 50% Central model was numerically lowest across model types, the improvement was not as great as expected based on the main effects alone. The 100% Central model had significantly improved performance on Central and Nord, but significantly worse performance on Balear, Nord-Occidental, and València. For the full model results, see Table 5 in Appendix C).

For the CER model, the same pattern of significance emerged for the main effects, but the interactions differed slightly. While the 20% Central model still had significantly higher performance on Balear and Nord-Occidental, its performance was significantly worse on Central test files. In addition, while the 50% model still had higher performance on Balear and València, it performed significantly worse on Central and Nord. The full results can be found in Table 6 in Appendix D.

Measured with WER and CER, the 50% Central model had a consistently strong performance across dialects, followed closely by the 20% Central model. Performance was generally higher for Central, Nord and Valencian dialects, but lower for the Balearic and Nord-Occidental dialects.

3.2 CW Attacks

We obtained a high percentage of successful attacks in all conditions (see Figure 1). The attacks' high average SNR implies that successful attacks were relatively imperceptible (see Tables 3 and 4). Given that our models had relatively low WER and CER on the non-adversarial test set, these results are in line with the common finding in the adversarial attack literature that even high-performing models are susceptible to adversarial perturbations. The logistic regression yielded no significant main effects and only one significant interaction, indicating that adversarial attacks using Central Catalan audio were significantly less successful in the 80% Central model relative to main effects alone. For the full model results, see Table 7 in Appendix E).

4 Discussion

In the present study, we manipulated the balance of five different dialects of Catalan in a dataset that we used to fine-tune XLSR-53 for automatic speech recognition. We tested how biasing a dataset toward one variety (Central Catalan) would affect the robustness of the model to both dialect variation and targeted adversarial noise at inference.

With respect to ASR performance on multiple dialects, we found that including larger portions of different dialects in fine-tuning data does make for a model that is more robust to dialect variation at test time. However, it is not necessary for a model to be perfectly balanced with respect to dialect composition to obtain maximal gains in performance. Other researchers have studied how to make models that are more robust to dialect variation at test time, for instance focusing on the config-

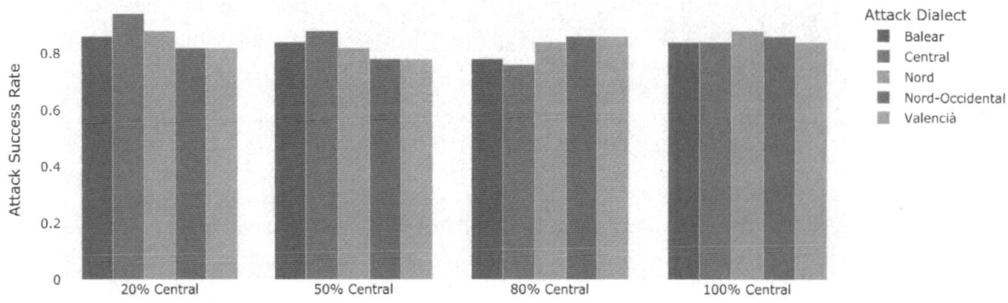

Figure 1: Attack success rate broken down by the dialect of the attack's audio (bar color) and the proportion of Central Catalan in the models' fine-tuning data (bar group).

uration of language models used during decoding (Yadavalli et al., 2022), the usefulness of normalizing dialects' scripts in the training data (Nigmatulina et al., 2020), or the utility of jointly learning to identify the variety and perform ASR for it (Waheed et al., 2023). While our experiments required relatively large amounts of data for which we knew the dialect of origin, we were encouraged about the implications of the results for low-resource dialect settings, as we see that even if half of the fine-tuning data used is from a single dialect, we can still observe substantial ASR improvements in performance for various dialects. Similar to a related study on the impact of balanced corpora on multi-dialect Irish ASR, we found that a perfectly balanced fine-tuning corpus does not lead to equivalent performance across dialects (Lonergan et al., 2023). Indeed, in our perfectly balanced model, the Balearic dialect stands out as having a relatively high WER (though the CER scores indicate closer performance across dialects). As suggested by Lonergan et al. (2023), this implies that the Balearic dialect may need to be up-sampled in future corpus compilation efforts.

As for adversarial noise, our results indicate that systematically adding dialect variation to fine-tuning data for ASR is neither helpful nor hurtful in the case of XLSR-53. Though CW attacks have previously been shown to be powerful against ASR systems, it is still interesting to consider if there were any parts of our experiments that made the models particularly vulnerable to the attacks. One potential susceptibility may be the presence of noisy labels in the training data. Paleka and Sanyal (2023) demonstrate that mislabeled images in training data can result in a loss of adversarial robustness for image classification models. We restricted our datasets to the validated text-audio pairs of Catalan data in Common Voice 18.0, and sentences contributed to the dataset for Catalan have undergone substantial validation (Armentano-Oller et al., 2024). Still, there is no guarantee that the dialect of the sentence matches the accent with which the reader speaks Catalan in the dataset. For instance, in our test set, we see a reader who speaks Valencià was assigned a sentence containing the feminine, third-person possessive pronoun from Central Catalan, "la seva." In Valencià, however, it is written and spoken as "la seua" (Calvo and Segura-Llopes, 2022), which is what our 100% Central Catalan model transcribes for this data point. Thus, it is feasible that there is inconsistency in our data's labels (the text) and what is actually spoken in the audio. A study of how languages' orthographic transparency impacts adversarial vulnerability in ASR models would be an interesting means of exploring the impact of such noisy labels.

5 Conclusion

Taking Catalan as the language of study given the large amounts of available annotated data, this study demonstrated that a more balanced dialect composition indeed confers robustness to dialect variation in test data. However, dialect composition of the training data had little influence on adversarial robustness. We hope that these findings will motivate the consideration of datasets' dialect composition in the development of ASR systems in the future. Indeed, our findings suggest that even if the dialects present in training are not perfectly balanced, including such variation to some degree is beneficial for *all* dialects represented in the training data (even for Central Catalan, in this case). As for adversarial robustness, we encourage further work on multilingual and multi-dialect speech processing models to assess specific vulnerabilities that might come from unbalanced datasets or mismatched labels and audio that spur from orthographic depth or dialect variation.

Limitations

Given that languages' dialects can differ in their mutual intelligibility, an important limitation arises in the use of only Catalan's varieties. It may be the case that for a language with less mutually intelligible dialects, less cross-dialect transfer is possible. Though we predict this would make for worse performance on lower resource dialects in the biased dataset conditions, more work on a larger sample of languages is needed. Collecting such multilingual, transcribed speech datasets with accent annotations presents a limitation in itself to this line of work. However, this paper and Zuluaga-Gomez et al. (2023)—who use Common Voice to create such a multiilingual dataset with accent labels—demonstrate that in some cases, existing datasets can be repurposed to study multi-dialect speech processing.

As we worked with limited computational resources, we were only able to fine-tune one time per data composition. Ideally, we would repeat the fine-tuning with several random samples and report the average results, but this was not feasible here. We encourage repetition of our experiments using other ASR architectures, including larger versions of XLSR, and with other languages and their dialects.

Ethical Considerations

This work studies adversarial attacks on automatic speech recognition, which could potentially be used to alter the behavior of ASR models with malicious intentions. We do not introduce any new algorithms for attacking models, and conducted the study with the intent of studying if multi-dialect speech processing models are more or less susceptible to existing attacks. In doing so, we hoped to assess not just the quality, but also the trustworthiness of speech recognition models that could potentially be used by speakers of lower-resource language varieties.

Acknowledgements

This research was supported by SNSF Grant PR00P1_208460 to EC.

References

Rosana Ardila, Megan Branson, Kelly Davis, Michael Kohler, Josh Meyer, Michael Henretty, Reuben Morais, Lindsay Saunders, Francis Tyers, and Gregor Weber. 2020. Common Voice: A massively-multilingual speech corpus. In *Proceedings of the Twelfth Language Resources and Evaluation Conference*, pages 4218–4222, Marseille, France. European Language Resources Association.

Carme Armentano-Oller, Montserrat Marimon, and Marta Villegas. 2024. Becoming a high-resource language in speech: The Catalan case in the Common Voice corpus. In *Proceedings of the 2024 Joint International Conference on Computational Linguistics, Language Resources and Evaluation (LREC-COLING 2024)*, pages 2142–2148.

Arun Babu, Changhan Wang, Andros Tjandra, Kushal Lakhotia, Qiantong Xu, Naman Goyal, Kritika Singh, Patrick Platen, Yatharth Saraf, Juan Pino, Alexei Baevski, Alexis Conneau, and Michael Auli. 2022. XLS-R: Self-supervised cross-lingual speech representation learning at scale. In *Interspeech, 2022*, pages 2278–2282.

Gemma Boleda, Stefan Bott, Rodrigo Meza, Carlos Castillo, Toni Badia, and Vicente López. 2006. CUCWeb: A Catalan corpus built from the web. In *Proceedings of the 2nd International Workshop on Web as Corpus*.

Vicent Beltran Calvo and Carles Segura-Llopes. 2022. *Els parlars valencians (actualitzada)*, volume 34. Universitat de València.

Nicholas Carlini and David Wagner. 2018. Audio adversarial examples: Targeted attacks on speech-to-text. In *2018 IEEE Security and Privacy Workshops (SPW)*, pages 1–7. IEEE.

Alexis Conneau, Alexei Baevski, Ronan Collobert, Abdelrahman Mohamed, and Michael Auli. 2021. Unsupervised cross-lingual representation learning for speech recognition. In *Interspeech, 2021*.

Zhengjia Dan, Yue Zhao, Xiaojun Bi, Licheng Wu, and Qiang Ji. 2022. Multi-task transformer with adaptive cross-entropy loss for multi-dialect speech recognition. *Entropy*, 24(10):1429.

Alex Graves, Santiago Fernández, Faustino Gomez, and Jürgen Schmidhuber. 2006. Connectionist temporal classification: labelling unsegmented sequence data with recurrent neural networks. In *Proceedings of the*

23rd international conference on Machine learning, pages 369–376.

Zhou Jie, Gao Shengxiang, Yu Zhengtao, Dong Ling, and Wang Wenjun. 2024. DialectMoE: An end-to-end multi-dialect speech recognition model with mixture-of-experts. In *Proceedings of the 23rd Chinese National Conference on Computational Linguistics (Volume 1: Main Conference)*, pages 1148–1159.

Diederik P. Kingma and Jimmy Ba. 2015. Adam: A method for stochastic optimization. In *3rd International Conference on Learning Representations, ICLR 2015, San Diego, CA, USA, May 7-9, 2015, Conference Track Proceedings*.

Oddur Kjartansson, Alexander Gutkin, Alena Butryna, Isin Demirsahin, and Clara Rivera. 2020. Open-source high quality speech datasets for Basque, Catalan and Galician. In *Proceedings of the 1st Joint Workshop on Spoken Language Technologies for Under-resourced languages (SLTU) and Collaboration and Computing for Under-Resourced Languages (CCURL)*, pages 21–27.

Baybars Kulebi, Carme Armentano-Oller, Carlos Rodriguez-Penagos, and Marta Villegas. 2022. ParlamentParla: A speech corpus of Catalan parliamentary sessions. In *Proceedings of the Workshop ParlaCLARIN III within the 13th Language Resources and Evaluation Conference*, pages 125–130, Marseille, France. European Language Resources Association.

Nikola Ljubešić and Antonio Toral. 2014. caWaC – a web corpus of Catalan and its application to language modeling and machine translation. In *Proceedings of the Ninth International Conference on Language Resources and Evaluation (LREC'14)*, pages 1728–1732, Reykjavik, Iceland. European Language Resources Association (ELRA).

Liam Lonergan, Mengjie Qian, Neasa Ní Chiaráin, Christer Gobl, and Ailbhe Ní Chasaide. 2023. Towards dialect-inclusive recognition in a low-resource language: Are balanced corpora the answer? In *Interspeech 2023*, pages 5082–5086.

Iuliia Nigmatulina, Tannon Kew, and Tanja Samardzic. 2020. ASR for non-standardised languages with dialectal variation: the case of Swiss German. In *Proceedings of the 7th Workshop on NLP for Similar Languages, Varieties and Dialects*, pages 15–24, Barcelona, Spain (Online). International Committee on Computational Linguistics (ICCL).

Raphaël Olivier and Bhiksha Raj. 2023. There is more than one kind of robustness: Fooling Whisper with adversarial examples. In *24th Annual Conference of the International Speech Communication Association, Interspeech 2023, Dublin, Ireland, August 20-24, 2023*, pages 4394–4398.

Daniel Paleka and Amartya Sanyal. 2023. A law of adversarial risk, interpolation, and label noise. In *The Eleventh International Conference on Learning Representations, ICLR 2023, Kigali, Rwanda, May 1-5, 2023*.

Luke E Richards, Edward Raff, and Cynthia Matuszek. 2023. Measuring equality in machine learning security defenses: A case study in speech recognition. In *Proceedings of the 16th ACM Workshop on Artificial Intelligence and Security*, pages 161–171.

Samuel Henrique Silva and Peyman Najafirad. 2020. Opportunities and challenges in deep learning adversarial robustness: A survey. *CoRR*.

Joan Veny. 1982. *Els parlars catalans: síntesi de dialectologia*. Biblioteca 'Raixa'. Moll.

Joan Veny. 2015. Català occidental/català oriental, encara. *Estudis Romànics*, 37:31–65.

Abdul Waheed, Bashar Talafha, Peter Sullivan, AbdelRahim Elmadany, and Muhammad Abdul-Mageed. 2023. VoxArabica: A robust dialect-aware arabic speech recognition system. In *Proceedings of ArabicNLP 2023, Singapore (Hybrid), December 7, 2023*, pages 441–449. Association for Computational Linguistics.

Tong Wu, Ziwei Liu, Qingqiu Huang, Yu Wang, and Dahua Lin. 2021. Adversarial robustness under long-tailed distribution. In *Proceedings of the IEEE/CVF Conference on Computer Vision and Pattern Recognition*, pages 8659–8668.

Aditya Yadavalli, Ganesh Sai Mirishkar, and Anil Vuppala. 2022. Exploring the effect of dialect mismatched language models in Telugu automatic speech recognition. In *Proceedings of the 2022 Conference of the North American Chapter of the Association for Computational Linguistics: Human Language Technologies: Student Research Workshop*, pages 292–301, Hybrid: Seattle, Washington + Online. Association for Computational Linguistics.

Juan Zuluaga-Gomez, Sara Ahmed, Danielius Visockas, and Cem Subakan. 2023. Commonaccent: Exploring large acoustic pretrained models for accent classification based on common voice. *Interspeech 2023*.

A Fine-Tuning Details

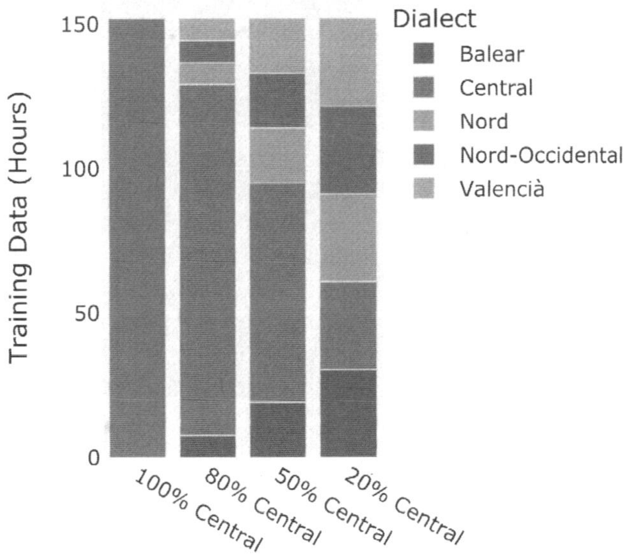

Figure 2: The proportion of five Catalan macro-dialects present in the training split of fine-tuning data for all four conditions.

To fine-tune XLSR-53 for Catalan ASR, we added a fully connected linear layer to the model that output logits over the vocabulary for each time step of the input audio. Similar to Conneau et al. (2021) and Babu et al. (2022), we used the connectionist temporal classification (CTC) loss function during training (Graves et al., 2006) and froze the weights in the model's CNN feature extractors. The audio files were resampled to the model sample rate and the text targets were tokenized into characters after decasing and removing punctuation. We retained any diacritics that are phonetically meaningful in Catalan and performed Unicode normalization so diacritics were represented consistently.

We trained with batch sizes of 16 but accumulated gradients for 16 batches before updating weights. Weight updates were made with the Adam optimizer (Kingma and Ba, 2015) and training continued until improvements to the development set loss were less than 0.05 for three epochs in a row. We found a stable learning rate of $9e^{-4}$ worked well across models. During inference, we used greedy decoding to transcribe input audio.

B CW Adversarial Attacks

B.1 Attack Training Algorithm

While training the adversarial noise, we set some upper limit ϵ to the value $|\delta_\infty|$. We then sought the perturbation δ for a given audio file x that minimized the CTC loss with respect to an adversarial target y while also keeping the noise's L_2 norm small. Thus, we aimed to minimize the following objective function:

$$\ell(x + \delta, y) + c|\delta|_2^2 \quad (2)$$

The constant c controls the relative importance of the regularizing term and therefore the noise's perceptibility. We iteratively calculated the objective in Equation 2 and updated the adversarial perturbation using the Adam optimizer. After every update to the noise, it was clamped such that $|\delta|_\infty \leq \epsilon$. Once a δ was found that successfully outputs the adversarial target y (as measured by a word error rate of 0 between y and the model output), ϵ was multiplied by a term α which is smaller than one to reduce the search radius and look for a quieter perturbation that successfully attacked the model. This continued until the search space was reduced k times or until a maximum number of updates n was carried out. See Table 2 for a summary of the hyperparameters we used while fitting attacks. We largely based our values off of those by Olivier and Raj (2023), though we found a higher learning rate worked better for our models.

Initial ϵ	0.10
c	0.25
α	0.70
learning rate	0.10
k	8
n	2000

Table 2: Hyperparameters for training CW attacks.

B.2 Detailed CW Attack Results

	Success Rate	Average SNR
100% Central	0.852	35.62
80% Central	0.820	35.44
50% Central	0.820	34.21
20% Central	0.864	35.80

Table 3: Attack success rate and average signal-to-noise ratio among successful CW attacks, broken down by the proportion of Central Catalan in each model's fine-tuning data. A higher average SNR of the attack indicates that among the successful attacks, quieter perturbations could be used to attain a successful attack.

	Success Rate	Average SNR
bal	0.830	36.73
cen	0.855	35.03
nor	0.855	34.27
no-oc	0.830	35.97
val	0.825	34.85

Table 4: Attack success rate and average signal-to-noise ratio among successful CW attacks, broken down by dialect of the attack's audio. A higher average SNR of the attack indicates that among the successful attacks, quieter perturbations could be used to attain a successful attack; bal: Balearic, cen: Central, nor: Nord, no-oc: Nord-Occidental, val: Valencià.

C Gamma Regression Output for WER

	Estimate	Standard Error	p-value
Intercept	0.176	8.84e-04	<2e-16***
20% Central	-0.019	0.001	<2e-16***
50% Central	-0.027	0.001	<2e-16***
80% Central	0.002	0.002	0.121
100% Central	0.044	0.002	<2e-16***
Balearic	0.042	0.002	<2e-16***
Central	-0.025	0.002	<2e-16***
Nord	-0.019	0.002	<2e-16***
Nord-Occidental	0.015	0.002	3.00e-16***
València	-0.013	0.002	1.18e-15***
20% Central × Balearic	-0.010	0.003	0.002**
50% Central × Balearic	-0.010	0.003	0.001**
80% Central × Balearic	0.003	0.004	0.339
100% Central × Balearic	0.017	0.004	4.44e-05***
20% Central × Central	0.033	0.003	<2e-16***
50% Central × Central	0.017	0.003	1.70e-11***
80% Central × Central	-0.006	0.003	0.016*
100% Central × Central	-0.043	0.003	<2e-16***
20% Central × Nord	0.007	0.003	0.009**
50% Central × Nord	0.004	0.002	0.158
80% Central × Nord	1.66e-04	0.003	0.953
100% Central × Nord	-0.010	0.003	0.001**
20% Central × Nord-Occidental	-0.011	0.003	1.38e-04***
50% Central × Nord-Occidental	-2.82e-04	0.003	0.923
80% Central × Nord-Occidental	0.002	0.003	0.468
100% Central × Nord-Occidental	0.009	0.003	0.018*
20% Central × València	-0.018	0.002	4.39e-13***
50% Central × València	-0.010	0.002	1.20e-04***
80% Central × València	4.23e-04	0.003	0.883
100% Central × València	0.027	0.004	5.27e-14***

Table 5: β estimates, standard errors, and p-values of the gamma regression predicting WER. Factors are sum-coded. *: significant at threshold 0.05; **: significant at threshold 0.01; ***: significant at threshold 0.001.

D Gamma Regression Output for CER

	Estimate	Standard Error	p-value
Intercept	0.045	2.81e-04	<2e-16***
20% Central	-0.004	4.51e-04	<2e-16***
50% Central	-0.008	4.26e-04	<2e-16***
80% Central	-1.14e-05	4.81e-04	0.981
100% Central	0.012	5.74e-04	<2e-16***
Balearic	0.014	6.87e-04	<2e-16***
Central	-0.007	4.86e-04	<2e-16***
Nord	-0.005	5.04e-04	<2e-16***
Nord-Occidental	0.004	5.94e-04	3.18e-13***
Valencià	-0.006	5.10e-04	<2e-16***
20% Central × Balearic	-0.005	0.001	4.75e-07***
50% Central × Balearic	-0.004	0.001	1.17e-04***
80% Central × Balearic	0.001	0.001	0.215
100% Central × Balearic	0.008	0.001	5.40e-08***
20% Central × Central	0.009	8.69e-04	<2e-16***
50% Central × Central	0.005	7.79e-04	8.61e-12***
80% Central × Central	-0.001	8.24e-04	0.090
100% Central × Central	-0.013	8.90e-04	<2e-16***
20% Central × Nord	6.69e-04	8.16e-04	0.413
50% Central × Nord	0.002	7.73e-04	0.040*
80% Central × Nord	5.00e-04	8.71e-04	0.566
100% Central × Nord	-0.003	0.001	0.007**
20% Central × Nord-Occidental	-0.003	9.31e-04	9.82e-04***
50% Central × Nord-Occidental	-9.45e-05	9.08e-04	0.917
80% Central × Nord-Occidental	3.55e-04	0.001	0.728
100% Central × Nord-Occidental	0.003	0.001	0.022*
20% Central × Valencià	-9.33e-04	8.02e-04	0.244
50% Central × Valencià	-0.003	7.34e-04	9.39e-05***
80% Central × Valencià	-9.45e-04	8.57e-04	0.270
100% Central × Valencià	0.005	0.001	1.47e-05***

Table 6: β estimates, standard errors, and p-values of the gamma regression predicting CER. Factors are sum-coded. *: significant at threshold 0.05; **: significant at threshold 0.01; ***: significant at threshold 0.001.

E Logistic Regression Output for CW Attacks

	Estimate	Standard Error	p-value
Intercept	1.689	0.089	<2e-16***
20% Central	0.229	0.166	0.168
50% Central	-0.149	0.149	0.316
80% Central	-0.148	0.149	0.321
100% Central	0.067	0.155	0.663
Balearic	-0.09	0.172	0.603
Central	0.200	0.195	0.306
Nord	0.101	0.181	0.578
Nord-Occidental	-0.086	0.173	0.620
Valencià	-0.125	0.171	0.465
20% Central × Balearic	-0.013	0.315	0.966
50% Central × Balearic	0.208	0.298	0.484
80% Central × Balearic	-0.186	0.281	0.508
100% Central × Balearic	-0.008	0.301	0.977
20% Central × Central	0.633	0.405	0.118
50% Central × Central	0.253	0.330	0.444
80% Central × Central	-0.588	0.292	0.044*
100% Central × Central	-0.298	0.314	0.343
20% Central × Nord	-0.027	0.331	0.935
50% Central × Nord	-0.124	0.296	0.675
80% Central × Nord	0.016	0.303	0.958
100% Central × Nord	0.135	0.325	0.678
20% Central × Nord-Occidental	-0.316	0.300	0.292
50% Central × Nord-Occidental	-0.188	0.281	0.503
80% Central × Nord-Occidental	0.360	0.306	0.240
100% Central × Nord-Occidental	0.145	0.309	0.640
20% Central × Valencià	-0.277	0.299	0.355
50% Central × Valencià	-0.149	0.280	0.595
80% Central × Valencià	0.399	0.305	0.191
100% Central × Valencià	0.027	0.300	0.929

Table 7: β estimates, standard errors, p-values of a logistic regression predicting adversarial attack success. Factors are sum-coded. *: significant at threshold 0.05; ***: significant at threshold 0.001.

The Impact of Dialect Variation on Robust Automatic Speech Recognition for Catalan

Zachary Hopton and **Eleanor Chodroff**
{zacharywilliam.hopton,eleanor.chodroff}@uzh.ch
University of Zurich

Abstract

To accurately transcribe a speech signal, automatic speech recognition (ASR) systems must show robustness to a wide range of task-independent variation, such as speaker factors, recording quality, or even "adversarial noise" designed to disrupt performance.We manipulated the dialect composition of fine-tuning data for ASR to study whether balancing the relative proportion of dialects had an impact on models' robustness to two such sources of variation: dialect variation and adversarial perturbations. We fine-tuned XLSR-53 for Catalan ASR using four different dialect compositions, each containing the Central Catalan dialect. These were defined as 100%, 80%, 50%, and 20% Central Catalan, with the remaining portions split evenly between four other Catalan dialects. While increasing the relative proportion of dialect variants improved models' dialect robustness, this did not have a meaningful impact on adversarial robustness. These findings suggest that while improvements to ASR can be made by diversifying the training data, such changes do not sufficiently counteract adversarial attacks, leaving the technology open to security threats.

https://github.com/zhopto3/DialAttack

1 Introduction

Effectively handling dialect variation is an important attribute of a high-performing automatic speech recognition system. While incorporating dialect variation into a model's training data may benefit this robustness (Jie et al., 2024; Dan et al., 2022; Lonergan et al., 2023), the relative lack of speech data with clean accent or dialect labels poses a challenge for this line of research. Moreover, the exact approach to incorporating data from other dialects could have consequences beyond just the model's ASR performance. Research on the robustness of neural networks to adversarial attacks has indicated that unbalanced training datasets may result in models that are more susceptible to adversarial attacks (Wu et al., 2021; Richards et al., 2023). When evaluating the susceptibility of Open AI's Whisper to adversarial noise, Olivier and Raj (2023) found that attacks on the model's language identification token were more effective when the attack's language was less present in the model's training data. For models trained on data from mutually intelligible dialects, it is an open question as to whether an unbalanced dataset would increase susceptibility to adversarial attacks. Training on multiple dialects may even confer a robustness to adversarial noise, analogous to training models on geometrically transformed or adversarial examples (Silva and Najafirad, 2020).

Catalan's well-documented dialect variation makes it a good candidate for studying questions of multi-dialect ASR (Veny, 2015, 1982; Calvo and Segura-Llopes, 2022). A great deal of research has focused on the compilation of Catalan corpora (Kjartansson et al., 2020; Kulebi et al., 2022; Boleda et al., 2006; Ljubešić and Toral, 2014). Catalan also has a substantial presence in the Common Voice corpus, for which diverse speakers of the language write, record, and validate data points on a voluntary basis (Ardila et al., 2020). Catalan's presence in Common Voice has grown substantially in recent releases of the corpus thanks to data management and campaigning efforts from a number of bodies (Armentano-Oller et al., 2024). Notable among these efforts is the encouragement of Catalan speakers with various accents to contribute to the corpus, and to include their accent in the metadata of the recording.

Here we use data from five Catalan dialects to answer two questions about multi-dialect ASR: First, to what extent is balancing the quantity of data from different dialects necessary when training models meant to accurately transcribe multiple varieties of a language? And second, does training an ASR

Proceedings of the The 22nd SIGMORPHON workshop on Computational Morphology, Phonology, and Phonetics, pages 34–44
May 3, 2025 ©2025 Association for Computational Linguistics

model on an unbalanced dataset with multiple dialects impact the model's security at inference?

2 Methods

2.1 Multi-dialect Catalan Speech Recognition

The first step of our experiments consisted of fine-tuning XLSR-53 for Catalan ASR (Conneau et al., 2021). We used XLSR-53 instead of a later version of XLSR since Catalan was not part of the pretraining data for this model, eliminating a potential confound in the manipulation of the dialect composition in the fine-tuning data[1].

Our data source was the validated portion of Catalan Common Voice 18.0[2] (Ardila et al., 2020). Similar to Armentano-Oller et al. (2024), we first mapped each unique accent label for a given audio file to one of five Catalan macro-dialects: Balearic, Central, Nord, Nord-Occidental, and Valencià. Audio files from second language learners were excluded, as were underspecified accent responses such as "Catalan" or "normative."

We then sampled four training and development datasets with 100%, 80%, 50%, and 20% Central Catalan; the remaining portion of each set was split evenly between the other four dialects. This meant that the 20% Central train and development datasets were perfectly balanced with respect to the five macro-dialects studied. We randomly sampled a single test set from the remaining data with an equal number of samples from each macro-dialect. Figure 2 shows the final proportion of each dialect in the four models' training data. All four models were fine-tuned on 152 hours of data with 19 hours of development data. This training set size is comparable to previous work that has used XLSR for multi-dialect speech processing (Zuluaga-Gomez et al., 2023; Lonergan et al., 2023). See Appendix A for fine-tuning details.

2.2 Robustness to Adversarial Noise

After training our ASR models, we randomly selected 50 audio files from each dialect's evaluation set to train a total of 250 adversarial attacks on each of the four models. Put generally, we aimed to add noise to our input audio files that resulted in the model outputting an adversarial target—"Porta'm a un lloc web malvat," or "Take me to an evil website"—despite the perceivable audio input saying something else. More specifically, we trained targeted, adversarial noise δ for a given audio file x as in Carlini and Wagner (2018). In such Carlini-and-Wagner (CW) attacks, the objective is also to make the noise relatively imperceptible. As in Olivier and Raj (2023), we judged the perceptibility of the noise relative to the signal in decibels using the signal-to-noise ratio (SNR), but using the L_∞ metric, similar to Carlini and Wagner (2018):

$$\mathrm{SNR}(x, \delta) = 20(\log |x|_\infty - \log |\delta|_\infty) \quad (1)$$

For details on the algorithm and hyperparameters used to train the adversarial noise δ, see Appendix B.

2.3 Evaluation

Following fine-tuning, we ran inference over the withheld test set of Catalan data. Each ASR model was evaluated on the same 19-hour evaluation dataset with equal representation from each dialect (2486 audio files per dialect).

To assess variation in WER and CER, a generalized linear model for a gamma-distributed dependent variable was implemented in R, using the identity link function. The model included main effects of the model dialect composition (100%, 80%, 50%, or 20% Central Catalan), the speech input dialect (Balear, Central, Nord, Nord-Occidental, or Valencià), and the interaction between the model dialect composition and speech dialect. A gamma distribution was chosen given that the WER and CER distributions have a strong positive skew and cannot be negative.[3] Each predictor was sum-coded with the held-out levels first set to the 100% Central model and the Catalan test files, and then rotated to test each main effect and interaction against the average performance.

To evaluate the effectiveness of the CW attacks on each fine-tuned model, we primarily use the percentage of successful attacks. An attack was considered successful if—at any SNR—the WER of the model output compared to the adversarial target ("Porta'm a un lloc web malvat.") was 0. To assess the influences on a successful or unsuccessful attack, we implemented a binomial logistic regression model with fixed effects of dialect, the fine-tuning data composition of the model, and

[1]https://github.com/facebookresearch/fairseq/tree/main/examples/wav2vec

[2]https://commonvoice.mozilla.org/en/datasets

[3]As the gamma prediction can only predict positive values greater than 0, we transformed any WER or CER of 0 in our data to 0.00001.

	WER					CER				
	bal	cen	nor	no-oc	val	bal	cen	nor	no-oc	val
100%	0.280	0.152	0.191	0.244	0.234	0.079	0.038	0.049	0.064	0.056
80%	0.224	0.146	0.160	0.196	0.165	0.060	0.037	0.040	0.050	0.039
50%	**0.181**	**0.140**	**0.133**	0.164	0.126	**0.047**	**0.035**	**0.033**	**0.041**	**0.029**
20%	0.189	0.164	0.144	**0.161**	**0.125**	0.050	0.043	0.036	0.042	0.035

Table 1: Percentages in the far left column represent the percent Central Catalan data used in fine-tuning; bal: Balearic, cen: Central, nor: Nord, no-oc: Nord-Occidental, val: Valencià; Bold: lowest WER/CER for each dialect.

their interaction. Categorical predictors were sum-coded.

3 Results

3.1 ASR

In terms of WER and CER, ASR for all dialects improved with more dialect-balanced data (Table 1). The WER model revealed significant influences of model composition and dialect input: relative to average, the 20% and 50% Central models had significantly lower WERs, while the 100% Central model had significantly higher WERs across all dialects. The average performance across models was significantly better on Central, Nord and Valencià, but worse on Balear and Nord-Occidental. The main effects were significantly tempered in several interactions; a significant interaction can be interpreted as a significant modulation from the expected WER performance based on the main effects alone. Beyond the main effects, the 20% Central model performed significantly better on Balear, Nord-Occidental, and Valencià, but worse on Central and Nord. The 50% Central model also performed significantly better on Balear and Valencià, but the main effect of the 50% Central model was significantly tempered for the Central test files: While the Central WER of the 50% Central model was numerically lowest across model types, the improvement was not as great as expected based on the main effects alone. The 100% Central model had significantly improved performance on Central and Nord, but significantly worse performance on Balear, Nord-Occidental, and Valencià. For the full model results, see Table 5 in Appendix C).

For the CER model, the same pattern of significance emerged for the main effects, but the interactions differed slightly. While the 20% Central model still had significantly higher performance on Balear and Nord-Occidental, its performance was significantly worse on Central test files. In addition, while the 50% model still had higher performance on Balear and Valencià, it performed significantly worse on Central and Nord. The full results can be found in Table 6 in Appendix D.

Measured with WER and CER, the 50% Central model had a consistently strong performance across dialects, followed closely by the 20% Central model. Performance was generally higher for Central, Nord and Valencian dialects, but lower for the Balearic and Nord-Occidental dialects.

3.2 CW Attacks

We obtained a high percentage of successful attacks in all conditions (see Figure 1). The attacks' high average SNR implies that successful attacks were relatively imperceptible (see Tables 3 and 4). Given that our models had relatively low WER and CER on the non-adversarial test set, these results are in line with the common finding in the adversarial attack literature that even high-performing models are susceptible to adversarial perturbations. The logistic regression yielded no significant main effects and only one significant interaction, indicating that adversarial attacks using Central Catalan audio were significantly less successful in the 80% Central model relative to main effects alone. For the full model results, see Table 7 in Appendix E).

4 Discussion

In the present study, we manipulated the balance of five different dialects of Catalan in a dataset that we used to fine-tune XLSR-53 for automatic speech recognition. We tested how biasing a dataset toward one variety (Central Catalan) would affect the robustness of the model to both dialect variation and targeted adversarial noise at inference.

With respect to ASR performance on multiple dialects, we found that including larger portions of different dialects in fine-tuning data does make for a model that is more robust to dialect variation at test time. However, it is not necessary for a model to be perfectly balanced with respect to dialect composition to obtain maximal gains in performance. Other researchers have studied how to make models that are more robust to dialect variation at test time, for instance focusing on the config-

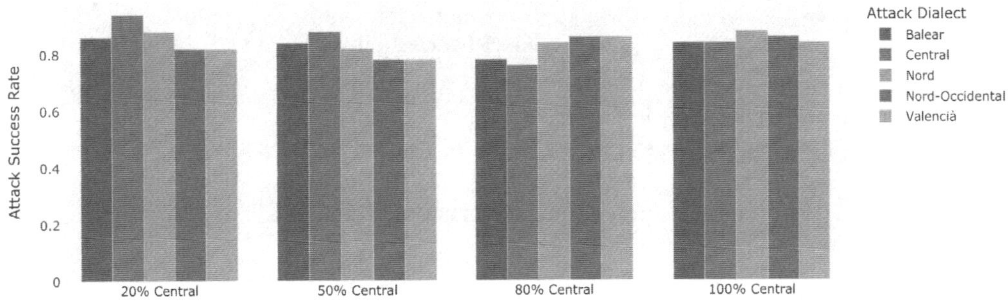

Figure 1: Attack success rate broken down by the dialect of the attack's audio (bar color) and the proportion of Central Catalan in the models' fine-tuning data (bar group).

uration of language models used during decoding (Yadavalli et al., 2022), the usefulness of normalizing dialects' scripts in the training data (Nigmatulina et al., 2020), or the utility of jointly learning to identify the variety and perform ASR for it (Waheed et al., 2023). While our experiments required relatively large amounts of data for which we knew the dialect of origin, we were encouraged about the implications of the results for low-resource dialect settings, as we see that even if half of the fine-tuning data used is from a single dialect, we can still observe substantial ASR improvements in performance for various dialects. Similar to a related study on the impact of balanced corpora on multi-dialect Irish ASR, we found that a perfectly balanced fine-tuning corpus does not lead to equivalent performance across dialects (Lonergan et al., 2023). Indeed, in our perfectly balanced model, the Balearic dialect stands out as having a relatively high WER (though the CER scores indicate closer performance across dialects). As suggested by Lonergan et al. (2023), this implies that the Balearic dialect may need to be up-sampled in future corpus compilation efforts.

As for adversarial noise, our results indicate that systematically adding dialect variation to fine-tuning data for ASR is neither helpful nor hurtful in the case of XLSR-53. Though CW attacks have previously been shown to be powerful against ASR systems, it is still interesting to consider if there were any parts of our experiments that made the models particularly vulnerable to the attacks. One potential susceptibility may be the presence of noisy labels in the training data. Paleka and Sanyal (2023) demonstrate that mislabeled images in training data can result in a loss of adversarial robustness for image classification models. We restricted our datasets to the validated text-audio pairs of Catalan data in Common Voice 18.0, and sentences contributed to the dataset for Catalan have undergone substantial validation (Armentano-Oller et al., 2024). Still, there is no guarantee that the dialect of the sentence matches the accent with which the reader speaks Catalan in the dataset. For instance, in our test set, we see a reader who speaks Valencià was assigned a sentence containing the feminine, third-person possessive pronoun from Central Catalan, "la seva." In Valencià, however, it is written and spoken as "la seua" (Calvo and Segura-Llopes, 2022), which is what our 100% Central Catalan model transcribes for this data point. Thus, it is feasible that there is inconsistency in our data's labels (the text) and what is actually spoken in the audio. A study of how languages' orthographic transparency impacts adversarial vulnerability in ASR models would be an interesting means of exploring the impact of such noisy labels.

5 Conclusion

Taking Catalan as the language of study given the large amounts of available annotated data, this study demonstrated that a more balanced dialect composition indeed confers robustness to dialect variation in test data. However, dialect composition of the training data had little influence on adversarial robustness. We hope that these findings will motivate the consideration of datasets' dialect composition in the development of ASR systems in the future. Indeed, our findings suggest that even if the dialects present in training are not perfectly balanced, including such variation to some degree is beneficial for *all* dialects represented in the training data (even for Central Catalan, in this case). As for adversarial robustness, we encourage further work on multilingual and multi-dialect speech processing models to assess specific vulnerabilities that might come from unbalanced datasets or mismatched labels and audio that spur from orthographic depth or dialect variation.

Limitations

Given that languages' dialects can differ in their mutual intelligibility, an important limitation arises in the use of only Catalan's varieties. It may be the case that for a language with less mutually intelligible dialects, less cross-dialect transfer is possible. Though we predict this would make for worse performance on lower resource dialects in the biased dataset conditions, more work on a larger sample of languages is needed. Collecting such multilingual, transcribed speech datasets with accent annotations presents a limitation in itself to this line of work. However, this paper and Zuluaga-Gomez et al. (2023)—who use Common Voice to create such a multiilingual dataset with accent labels—demonstrate that in some cases, existing datasets can be repurposed to study multi-dialect speech processing.

As we worked with limited computational resources, we were only able to fine-tune one time per data composition. Ideally, we would repeat the fine-tuning with several random samples and report the average results, but this was not feasible here. We encourage repetition of our experiments using other ASR architectures, including larger versions of XLSR, and with other languages and their dialects.

Ethical Considerations

This work studies adversarial attacks on automatic speech recognition, which could potentially be used to alter the behavior of ASR models with malicious intentions. We do not introduce any new algorithms for attacking models, and conducted the study with the intent of studying if multi-dialect speech processing models are more or less susceptible to existing attacks. In doing so, we hoped to assess not just the quality, but also the trustworthiness of speech recognition models that could potentially be used by speakers of lower-resource language varieties.

Acknowledgements

This research was supported by SNSF Grant PR00P1_208460 to EC.

References

Rosana Ardila, Megan Branson, Kelly Davis, Michael Kohler, Josh Meyer, Michael Henretty, Reuben Morais, Lindsay Saunders, Francis Tyers, and Gregor Weber. 2020. Common Voice: A massively-multilingual speech corpus. In *Proceedings of the Twelfth Language Resources and Evaluation Conference*, pages 4218–4222, Marseille, France. European Language Resources Association.

Carme Armentano-Oller, Montserrat Marimon, and Marta Villegas. 2024. Becoming a high-resource language in speech: The Catalan case in the Common Voice corpus. In *Proceedings of the 2024 Joint International Conference on Computational Linguistics, Language Resources and Evaluation (LREC-COLING 2024)*, pages 2142–2148.

Arun Babu, Changhan Wang, Andros Tjandra, Kushal Lakhotia, Qiantong Xu, Naman Goyal, Kritika Singh, Patrick Platen, Yatharth Saraf, Juan Pino, Alexei Baevski, Alexis Conneau, and Michael Auli. 2022. XLS-R: Self-supervised cross-lingual speech representation learning at scale. In *Interspeech, 2022*, pages 2278–2282.

Gemma Boleda, Stefan Bott, Rodrigo Meza, Carlos Castillo, Toni Badia, and Vicente López. 2006. CUCWeb: A Catalan corpus built from the web. In *Proceedings of the 2nd International Workshop on Web as Corpus*.

Vicent Beltran Calvo and Carles Segura-Llopes. 2022. *Els parlars valencians (actualitzada)*, volume 34. Universitat de València.

Nicholas Carlini and David Wagner. 2018. Audio adversarial examples: Targeted attacks on speech-to-text. In *2018 IEEE Security and Privacy Workshops (SPW)*, pages 1–7. IEEE.

Alexis Conneau, Alexei Baevski, Ronan Collobert, Abdelrahman Mohamed, and Michael Auli. 2021. Unsupervised cross-lingual representation learning for speech recognition. In *Interspeech, 2021*.

Zhengjia Dan, Yue Zhao, Xiaojun Bi, Licheng Wu, and Qiang Ji. 2022. Multi-task transformer with adaptive cross-entropy loss for multi-dialect speech recognition. *Entropy*, 24(10):1429.

Alex Graves, Santiago Fernández, Faustino Gomez, and Jürgen Schmidhuber. 2006. Connectionist temporal classification: labelling unsegmented sequence data with recurrent neural networks. In *Proceedings of the*

23rd international conference on Machine learning, pages 369–376.

Zhou Jie, Gao Shengxiang, Yu Zhengtao, Dong Ling, and Wang Wenjun. 2024. DialectMoE: An end-to-end multi-dialect speech recognition model with mixture-of-experts. In *Proceedings of the 23rd Chinese National Conference on Computational Linguistics (Volume 1: Main Conference)*, pages 1148–1159.

Diederik P. Kingma and Jimmy Ba. 2015. Adam: A method for stochastic optimization. In *3rd International Conference on Learning Representations, ICLR 2015, San Diego, CA, USA, May 7-9, 2015, Conference Track Proceedings*.

Oddur Kjartansson, Alexander Gutkin, Alena Butryna, Isin Demirsahin, and Clara Rivera. 2020. Open-source high quality speech datasets for Basque, Catalan and Galician. In *Proceedings of the 1st Joint Workshop on Spoken Language Technologies for Under-resourced languages (SLTU) and Collaboration and Computing for Under-Resourced Languages (CCURL)*, pages 21–27.

Baybars Kulebi, Carme Armentano-Oller, Carlos Rodriguez-Penagos, and Marta Villegas. 2022. ParlamentParla: A speech corpus of Catalan parliamentary sessions. In *Proceedings of the Workshop ParlaCLARIN III within the 13th Language Resources and Evaluation Conference*, pages 125–130, Marseille, France. European Language Resources Association.

Nikola Ljubešić and Antonio Toral. 2014. caWaC – a web corpus of Catalan and its application to language modeling and machine translation. In *Proceedings of the Ninth International Conference on Language Resources and Evaluation (LREC'14)*, pages 1728–1732, Reykjavik, Iceland. European Language Resources Association (ELRA).

Liam Lonergan, Mengjie Qian, Neasa Ní Chiaráin, Christer Gobl, and Ailbhe Ní Chasaide. 2023. Towards dialect-inclusive recognition in a low-resource language: Are balanced corpora the answer? In *Interspeech 2023*, pages 5082–5086.

Iuliia Nigmatulina, Tannon Kew, and Tanja Samardzic. 2020. ASR for non-standardised languages with dialectal variation: the case of Swiss German. In *Proceedings of the 7th Workshop on NLP for Similar Languages, Varieties and Dialects*, pages 15–24, Barcelona, Spain (Online). International Committee on Computational Linguistics (ICCL).

Raphaël Olivier and Bhiksha Raj. 2023. There is more than one kind of robustness: Fooling Whisper with adversarial examples. In *24th Annual Conference of the International Speech Communication Association, Interspeech 2023, Dublin, Ireland, August 20-24, 2023*, pages 4394–4398.

Daniel Paleka and Amartya Sanyal. 2023. A law of adversarial risk, interpolation, and label noise. In *The Eleventh International Conference on Learning Representations, ICLR 2023, Kigali, Rwanda, May 1-5, 2023*.

Luke E Richards, Edward Raff, and Cynthia Matuszek. 2023. Measuring equality in machine learning security defenses: A case study in speech recognition. In *Proceedings of the 16th ACM Workshop on Artificial Intelligence and Security*, pages 161–171.

Samuel Henrique Silva and Peyman Najafirad. 2020. Opportunities and challenges in deep learning adversarial robustness: A survey. *CoRR*.

Joan Veny. 1982. *Els parlars catalans: síntesi de dialectologia*. Biblioteca 'Raixa'. Moll.

Joan Veny. 2015. Català occidental/català oriental, encara. *Estudis Romànics*, 37:31–65.

Abdul Waheed, Bashar Talafha, Peter Sullivan, AbdelRahim Elmadany, and Muhammad Abdul-Mageed. 2023. VoxArabica: A robust dialect-aware arabic speech recognition system. In *Proceedings of ArabicNLP 2023, Singapore (Hybrid), December 7, 2023*, pages 441–449. Association for Computational Linguistics.

Tong Wu, Ziwei Liu, Qingqiu Huang, Yu Wang, and Dahua Lin. 2021. Adversarial robustness under long-tailed distribution. In *Proceedings of the IEEE/CVF Conference on Computer Vision and Pattern Recognition*, pages 8659–8668.

Aditya Yadavalli, Ganesh Sai Mirishkar, and Anil Vuppala. 2022. Exploring the effect of dialect mismatched language models in Telugu automatic speech recognition. In *Proceedings of the 2022 Conference of the North American Chapter of the Association for Computational Linguistics: Human Language Technologies: Student Research Workshop*, pages 292–301, Hybrid: Seattle, Washington + Online. Association for Computational Linguistics.

Juan Zuluaga-Gomez, Sara Ahmed, Danielius Visockas, and Cem Subakan. 2023. Commonaccent: Exploring large acoustic pretrained models for accent classification based on common voice. *Interspeech 2023*.

A Fine-Tuning Details

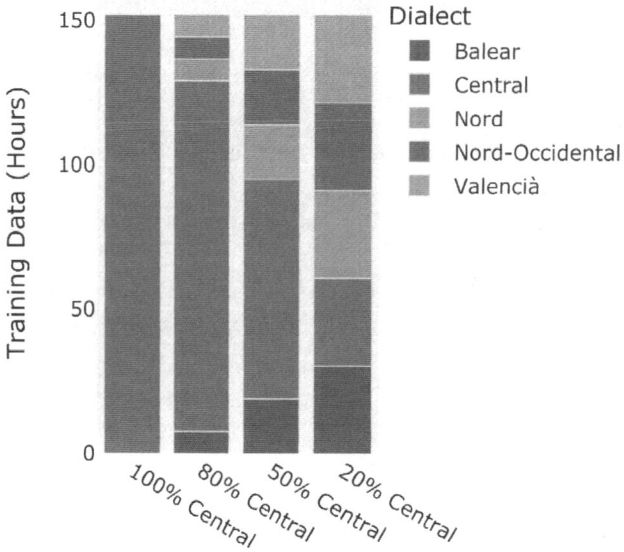

Figure 2: The proportion of five Catalan macro-dialects present in the training split of fine-tuning data for all four conditions.

To fine-tune XLSR-53 for Catalan ASR, we added a fully connected linear layer to the model that output logits over the vocabulary for each time step of the input audio. Similar to Conneau et al. (2021) and Babu et al. (2022), we used the connectionist temporal classification (CTC) loss function during training (Graves et al., 2006) and froze the weights in the model's CNN feature extractors. The audio files were resampled to the model sample rate and the text targets were tokenized into characters after decasing and removing punctuation. We retained any diacritics that are phonetically meaningful in Catalan and performed Unicode normalization so diacritics were represented consistently.

We trained with batch sizes of 16 but accumulated gradients for 16 batches before updating weights. Weight updates were made with the Adam optimizer (Kingma and Ba, 2015) and training continued until improvements to the development set loss were less than 0.05 for three epochs in a row. We found a stable learning rate of $9e^{-4}$ worked well across models. During inference, we used greedy decoding to transcribe input audio.

B CW Adversarial Attacks

B.1 Attack Training Algorithm

While training the adversarial noise, we set some upper limit ϵ to the value $|\delta_\infty|$. We then sought the perturbation δ for a given audio file x that minimized the CTC loss with respect to an adversarial target y while also keeping the noise's L_2 norm small. Thus, we aimed to minimize the following objective function:

$$\ell(x + \delta, y) + c|\delta|_2^2 \tag{2}$$

The constant c controls the relative importance of the regularizing term and therefore the noise's perceptibility. We iteratively calculated the objective in Equation 2 and updated the adversarial perturbation using the Adam optimizer. After every update to the noise, it was clamped such that $|\delta|_\infty \leq \epsilon$. Once a δ was found that successfully outputs the adversarial target y (as measured by a word error rate of 0 between y and the model output), ϵ was multiplied by a term α which is smaller than one to reduce the search radius and look for a quieter perturbation that successfully attacked the model. This continued until the search space was reduced k times or until a maximum number of updates n was carried out. See Table 2 for a summary of the hyperparameters we used while fitting attacks. We largely based our values off of those by Olivier and Raj (2023), though we found a higher learning rate worked better for our models.

Initial ϵ	0.10
c	0.25
α	0.70
learning rate	0.10
k	8
n	2000

Table 2: Hyperparameters for training CW attacks.

B.2 Detailed CW Attack Results

	Success Rate	Average SNR
100% Central	0.852	35.62
80% Central	0.820	35.44
50% Central	0.820	34.21
20% Central	0.864	35.80

Table 3: Attack success rate and average signal-to-noise ratio among successful CW attacks, broken down by the proportion of Central Catalan in each model's fine-tuning data. A higher average SNR of the attack indicates that among the successful attacks, quieter perturbations could be used to attain a successful attack.

	Success Rate	Average SNR
bal	0.830	36.73
cen	0.855	35.03
nor	0.855	34.27
no-oc	0.830	35.97
val	0.825	34.85

Table 4: Attack success rate and average signal-to-noise ratio among successful CW attacks, broken down by dialect of the attack's audio. A higher average SNR of the attack indicates that among the successful attacks, quieter perturbations could be used to attain a successful attack; bal: Balearic, cen: Central, nor: Nord, no-oc: Nord-Occidental, val: Valencià.

C Gamma Regression Output for WER

	Estimate	Standard Error	p-value
Intercept	0.176	8.84e-04	<2e-16***
20% Central	-0.019	0.001	<2e-16***
50% Central	-0.027	0.001	<2e-16***
80% Central	0.002	0.002	0.121
100% Central	0.044	0.002	<2e-16***
Balearic	0.042	0.002	<2e-16***
Central	-0.025	0.002	<2e-16***
Nord	-0.019	0.002	<2e-16***
Nord-Occidental	0.015	0.002	3.00e-16***
Valencià	-0.013	0.002	1.18e-15***
20% Central × Balearic	-0.010	0.003	0.002**
50% Central × Balearic	-0.010	0.003	0.001**
80% Central × Balearic	0.003	0.004	0.339
100% Central × Balearic	0.017	0.004	4.44e-05***
20% Central × Central	0.033	0.003	<2e-16***
50% Central × Central	0.017	0.003	1.70e-11***
80% Central × Central	-0.006	0.003	0.016*
100% Central × Central	-0.043	0.003	<2e-16***
20% Central × Nord	0.007	0.003	0.009**
50% Central × Nord	0.004	0.002	0.158
80% Central × Nord	1.66e-04	0.003	0.953
100% Central × Nord	-0.010	0.003	0.001**
20% Central × Nord-Occidental	-0.011	0.003	1.38e-04***
50% Central × Nord-Occidental	-2.82e-04	0.003	0.923
80% Central × Nord-Occidental	0.002	0.003	0.468
100% Central × Nord-Occidental	0.009	0.003	0.018*
20% Central × Valencià	-0.018	0.002	4.39e-13***
50% Central × Valencià	-0.010	0.002	1.20e-04***
80% Central × Valencià	4.23e-04	0.003	0.883
100% Central × Valencià	0.027	0.004	5.27e-14***

Table 5: β estimates, standard errors, and p-values of the gamma regression predicting WER. Factors are sum-coded. *: significant at threshold 0.05; **: significant at threshold 0.01; ***: significant at threshold 0.001.

D Gamma Regression Output for CER

	Estimate	Standard Error	p-value
Intercept	0.045	2.81e-04	<2e-16***
20% Central	-0.004	4.51e-04	<2e-16***
50% Central	-0.008	4.26e-04	<2e-16***
80% Central	-1.14e-05	4.81e-04	0.981
100% Central	0.012	5.74e-04	<2e-16***
Balearic	0.014	6.87e-04	<2e-16***
Central	-0.007	4.86e-04	<2e-16***
Nord	-0.005	5.04e-04	<2e-16***
Nord-Occidental	0.004	5.94e-04	3.18e-13***
València	-0.006	5.10e-04	<2e-16***
20% Central × Balearic	-0.005	0.001	4.75e-07***
50% Central × Balearic	-0.004	0.001	1.17e-04***
80% Central × Balearic	0.001	0.001	0.215
100% Central × Balearic	0.008	0.001	5.40e-08***
20% Central × Central	0.009	8.69e-04	<2e-16***
50% Central × Central	0.005	7.79e-04	8.61e-12***
80% Central × Central	-0.001	8.24e-04	0.090
100% Central × Central	-0.013	8.90e-04	<2e-16***
20% Central × Nord	6.69e-04	8.16e-04	0.413
50% Central × Nord	0.002	7.73e-04	0.040*
80% Central × Nord	5.00e-04	8.71e-04	0.566
100% Central × Nord	-0.003	0.001	0.007**
20% Central × Nord-Occidental	-0.003	9.31e-04	9.82e-04***
50% Central × Nord-Occidental	-9.45e-05	9.08e-04	0.917
80% Central × Nord-Occidental	3.55e-04	0.001	0.728
100% Central × Nord-Occidental	0.003	0.001	0.022*
20% Central × València	-9.33e-04	8.02e-04	0.244
50% Central × València	-0.003	7.34e-04	9.39e-05***
80% Central × València	-9.45e-04	8.57e-04	0.270
100% Central × València	0.005	0.001	1.47e-05***

Table 6: β estimates, standard errors, and p-values of the gamma regression predicting CER. Factors are sum-coded. *: significant at threshold 0.05; **: significant at threshold 0.01; ***: significant at threshold 0.001.

E Logistic Regression Output for CW Attacks

	Estimate	Standard Error	p-value
Intercept	1.689	0.089	<2e-16***
20% Central	0.229	0.166	0.168
50% Central	-0.149	0.149	0.316
80% Central	-0.148	0.149	0.321
100% Central	0.067	0.155	0.663
Balearic	-0.09	0.172	0.603
Central	0.200	0.195	0.306
Nord	0.101	0.181	0.578
Nord-Occidental	-0.086	0.173	0.620
Valencià	-0.125	0.171	0.465
20% Central × Balearic	-0.013	0.315	0.966
50% Central × Balearic	0.208	0.298	0.484
80% Central × Balearic	-0.186	0.281	0.508
100% Central × Balearic	-0.008	0.301	0.977
20% Central × Central	0.633	0.405	0.118
50% Central × Central	0.253	0.330	0.444
80% Central × Central	-0.588	0.292	0.044*
100% Central × Central	-0.298	0.314	0.343
20% Central × Nord	-0.027	0.331	0.935
50% Central × Nord	-0.124	0.296	0.675
80% Central × Nord	0.016	0.303	0.958
100% Central × Nord	0.135	0.325	0.678
20% Central × Nord-Occidental	-0.316	0.300	0.292
50% Central × Nord-Occidental	-0.188	0.281	0.503
80% Central × Nord-Occidental	0.360	0.306	0.240
100% Central × Nord-Occidental	0.145	0.309	0.640
20% Central × Valencià	-0.277	0.299	0.355
50% Central × Valencià	-0.149	0.280	0.595
80% Central × Valencià	0.399	0.305	0.191
100% Central × Valencià	0.027	0.300	0.929

Table 7: β estimates, standard errors, p-values of a logistic regression predicting adversarial attack success. Factors are sum-coded. *: significant at threshold 0.05; ***: significant at threshold 0.001.

Author Index